Scattered Thoughts
From a Scattered Mind

Scattered Thoughts
From a Scattered Mind

Volume XII
Tributary

David Mills

Library of Congress Control Number:		2019917164
ISBN:	Hardcover	979-8-3694-1070-7
	Softcover	979-8-3694-1069-1
	eBook	979-8-3694-1068-4

Print information available on the last page.

Rev. date: 11/08/2023

To order additional copies of this book, contact:
Xlibris
844-714-8691
www.Xlibris.com
Orders@Xlibris.com
856644

For Cathy Karen
who's laughter is my favorite sound

"Only a life lived for others is a life worthwhile."

Albert Einstein

"He became like us, so we could become like Him."

Max Lucado

CONTENTS

Foreword

Volume twelve. Go figure.

Sometime in the year of our Lord, 2011, I decided to round up all of my collected musings (going all the way back to high school) and publish them in a book.

I remember thinking, long before I decided to make this happen, that if I ever followed through, I would entitle it "Scattered Thoughts From a Scattered Mind."

I'm not sure, now so many years later, but my life-long friend Richard Parham might have been the one who encouraged me to use that title. "I like it!" He said, "Everyone will know who wrote it **before** your name appears at the bottom!"

We were and are, as the bible says, of one accord.

Though he has never been officially credited with such, his picture does grace the cover of volume one.

But I digress.

We are not here to talk about the long ago, but relish in the here and now.

And relish we shall in our twelfth offering, as our trained and certified guides lead us through another magical journey into the Land of Scattered Thoughts.

Please keep your seat belts securely fastened at all times and refrain from wandering about the cabin.

50

Twenty years apart, and yet we grew together,
You, a happy youth, giving it all you had,
Me, a restless surfer, learning to be your Dad.

We worked it out each day, one testing the other,
These the early days, long before your brothers.

The little house was home,
                          the yard was big and wide,
We stole some time together, hanging side-by side.

There were parties, holidays,
                          friends and dogs to boot,
With photos of it all, as life was taking root.

These the early days, long before your brothers,
Just the three of us, the cooking was your mothers'.

Baseball games, adventure trips,
          and Green Cove Springs returns,
Our life was like no other, easy, no concerns.

Memories galore, I remember them by name,
But time moves on for all of us,
                          and sometimes it's a shame.

But through it all, The Good Lord waits,
                  and watches as we grow,
He brings His riches with Him,
                  He's coming soon you know.

Twenty years apart, and yet we grew together,
The happy youth became a man,
                  and now his children's Dad,
The old man smiled and closed the file,
                  having given all he had.

For Rick Mills, of whom I am most proud…
50th birthday, December 2022

The Sound

The very last breath is precious,
                              it escapes with little sound,
A wonderful life that was, no longer can be found.

Absent from the body, now present with the Lord,
This scripture gives us comfort, the Living Word as poured.

I rest in He who penned it, I trust His promise too,
I speak it as good counsel, I pray it speaks to you.

The angels bound about, as a spirit starts it's floating,
Witnessing the sound, the sound of life now closing.

Rising

A single candle burns casting shadows on the wall,
Twenty-five or thirty if you stop to count them all.
Angels in the heavens as my mother used to say,
The Lord and all His legions
        making smooth and straight your way.

She often told me stories from the pages of His book,
Stories of His love for us, no matter where I'd look.
She said I'd live a lifetime and never find the end,
Of how He watches over me, my ever-lasting friend.

I often think about her,
        and the treasures she received,
As she made her way to heaven,
        to the glory she perceived.
I see her ever rising as the angels lead the way,
Her single candle melding
        with the millions on display.

Twilight Sky

Messin' around under twilight sky,
Headed for the cabin and a Montana high.
A short-armed ticket is the way we like to ride,
Coming home together, side by side.

Our life in the woods in calling us home,
Forty to the neighbor yet you're never alone.
The passion is ours but the payments are steep,
Still a half a day's ride to catch our sleep.

The horses are wild, the land untamed,
There are towns laid empty, many unnamed.
Not sure we can keep it, but we're sure gonna try,
Underneath the splendor of that twilight sky.

Halloween

A timely treat, or timidly trick?
A shoeless horn, or walking stick?
Another season some might say,
To hide away with Hemmingway.

I'll never know the difference now,
Or understand the sacred cow,
As fool and money soon part ways,
It's how the unschooled spend their days.

Another day in paradise,
The finished promise twice as nice,
I hate to bring it up again,
But told you this would never end.

So count your blessings, bless your count,
Never lose the war to doubt,
A troubled soul is value-less,
Our lives are shortened by the stress.

For James

Infectious smile, out-going pride,
The life he lived was Riley.
It tells the story as you know,
But not the tale entirely.

He passed so many years ago,
Announcements told us all.
Yet who could know among us,
He'd suffered only fall.

Heal he did and traveled on,
The path as laid before.
A soldier hidden in his heart,
Became his tour deforce.

Now he rests, his work is done,
He leaves us left to mourn.
Yet happy knowing James as friend,
As from our grasp he's torn.

for James Eugene Simmons
Classmate and friend
December 16, 1951 - February 11, 2023

Aging (Part II)

The countless days arrive at last,
We fall into the die as cast.
A prayer for those who've headed west,
A prayer for those of scheduled test.

He alone can count the days,
And save us from our sinful ways.
We love our families, our friends,
We pray these days will never end.

The love of life is strong indeed,
In we, the reared of Adam's seed.
We long for better days ahead,
Our prayer list scanned in infrared.

These the days arrive at last,
They come with special question asked.
If time expires before you wake,
Did you choose life or sad mistake?

Truth (Part II)

Going through those changes,
Getting older by the day.
Just trying to find some shelter,
A comfortable place to stay.

The Good Lord and His mercy,
Has watched me go this far.
He is my Lord, my Keeper,
My luminous Morning Star.

My mind is on Him always,
I am His child, His ward.
I see His face in trials,
We live in one accord.

I'll stand before Him one day,
And the tears of joy will flow.
He sent His Son to save me,
As His Spirit told me so.

Now death it has no hold on me,
No victory, no sting.
For I've received the truth of life,
That only Jesus brings.

The Better Life

Oh, to live the better life,
A better life than this!
One where sin rules not the day,
One where I resist!

For I the hapless sinner,
Am bound by chains, secure.
I long to free my troubled soul,
To live, just not endure.

Release me from my bondage,
Hear my prayer oh Lord.
Cleanse me from this heartache,
Bring your cross, your sword.

Pull this darkness from me,
Fill me with your light.
For on my own is failure,
So I'm giving you this fight.

You are the true and faithful,
The One to set me free.
For I the captive taken,
Will find myself in thee.

Prophet

Annoyed, he closed the book,
                   and cautioned us a stare,
The kind that foretells trouble,
                   fashioned from despair.

A snippet from the future, a prophesy of note,
As winter wrapped around the isle,
                   surrounding men and boat.

Alas, the times have changed,
                   the old school reigns no more.
We relish in our wisdom, unchanged, we hit the door.

We chisel out our days, without a thought or prayer,
We tilt our caps in honor to
                   "the man who lives upstairs."

Yet future tense comes quickly, contagion in us all,
A ways and means reduction,
                   stepping forward for the fall.

The cure is Christ alone, the Savior of us all,
Cut lose the ties that bind, and answer when He calls.

For David

Friends we are and friends we'll be,
No matter time nor age.
This book is not yet written,
So we'll write another page.

You are one of many,
My brothers from the street.
And to this day, our bond so strong,
Makes all of us complete.

I watched you handle trials,
So early in your life,
I watched you grow into a man,
Who serves his Lord, his wife.

I am so proud to call you friend,
To know you as I do.
And then to celebrate with you,
Long after this life ends.

For lifelong friend, David Stubbs
on his 70th birthday, March 2023

Sixty-Nine

Sixty-nine and oh, so fine,
A carousel of pleasure.
You make me happy every day,
Refreshed, by any measure.

Hour by hour, day by day,
My thoughts are on you often.
The joy of you infects me so,
This hardened heart, you've softened.

Thank you little Yankee girl,
For making me your man.
When others fall and stumble,
I know we'll make a stand.

I'll wish you happy birthday,
I'll wish you many more.
I know the Good Lord guides us now,
I want to see much more!

For my wife, Cathy Karen, with love.
June 2023

Eventually

Eventually, the grieving wind, and with it,
                                    rain will come,
A time of true rebellion, a time to come undone.

The wistfulness of youth, a pipe-assisted journey,
Rescues rhyme and reason, reveals a past unworthy.

I bathe in setting sun, the sky alive in color,
Creation at its best, a landscape like no other.

Redemption stands a task, a welcome unmade bed,
I hear the spirits groan, accusations from the dead.

A darkened world resides,
                            the lake as blackened tomb,
The winter sky applauds another
                                    emptied, tempered womb.

I whisper yet your name as night envelopes me,
A statue of ineptness, for all the world to see.

One Year In

One year in and good so far,
Much smoother than your little car.

We've had our bumps and bruises too,
Yet set our minds to see it through.

The Good Lord knows our wants, our needs,
We'll follow Him and dodge the weeds.

Our love is real and worth the task,
To find resolve, to make it last.

We'll turn the page, begin year two,
I'll watch it grow, my love for you!

For Cathy Karen
First Anniversary
May 2023

Fifty on the Nose

This is the story of David and Beth,
A union styled to pass the test.

Of time and testing, trials galore,
A story mired in American lore.

They met as teens and married young,
And soon a family was begun.

They went to work and worked real hard,
Remodeled their homes and mowed their yards.

Children came, a girl, then another,
As fortune would have it, never a brother.

But never you mind, these four musketeers,
Loved one another and grew through the years.

Now Heather and Jenny have kids of their own,
And David and Beth wonder,
                    "Where has time flown?"

The Good Book will tell us that life is a mist,
Traceable back to that first good kiss.

Before you know it, it's fifty good years,
And you're out on a boat with a car-load of peers.

So David and Beth, we celebrate you,
And the union you've made
                        with some mighty fine glue!

For my good friends David and Beth Stubbs
50th Anniversary
July 2023

The Legend of Ruth Bartel

She threw the tomahawk at twelve,
                    wrestled bears at twenty,
She has a favorite candy,
                    they call it "Good and Plenty".

She voted prohibition, then ran midnight shine.
The revenuers chased her,
                    but she left them far behind.

When she fell a while ago,
                    the buzzards licked their lips,
She only wished she'd worn her belt,
                    her pistols on her hips.

She's one of a kind, our birthday girl,
And we wouldn't trade her for half the known world.

He name is Ruth, like the bible tells,
And she lives in the country where her family dwells.

So we've gathered together to wish her our best,
Through many a trial, she's passed each test.

The Good Lord in time will hand her a crown,
Where His light now shines and His Angels abound.

Ocean Cay

A cloud bank hides the sand dune,
                and with it setting sun,
As darkness sweeps across the bay,
                I sign the letter; come.

A single candle lights the room, my tablet sits at ease,
I edit what I've proffered, I change it as I please.

For she remains a mystery, but often welcome muse,
Who makes me tend my garden,
                and render up my dues.

She's trouble and she's talent, a whirlwind in a dress,
She leaves me tired and winded, I seldom get my rest.

All who know her love her,
                her texts, her cards, her notes,
They come together sweetly,
                like jam and buttered toast.

She is the better half, she reminds me of my duty,
The Good Lord sent a treat
                in this blue-eyed, redhead beauty.

We'll live our lives together,

                  the work, the trips, the fun,

We'll put a dozen in the books, and only just begun.

Ocean Cay
MSC Cruise line private island
July 2023

Tributary

Countless hours, endless days,
Life absorbed in flight delays.

I wish I may, I wish I might,
Make the yellow traffic light.

Life at speed, tomorrow's print,
Who can master without hint?

We the weary, want to know,
Is it real, or just a show?

Feed the piper, play the game,
It sometimes seems it's all the same.

Yet we serve Him who set the post,
Who guides us with His Holy Ghost.

His word prevails, His power reigns,
The Lord of Hosts, unlocked the chains,

That held us captive, bound by sin,
Our hope, our faith is now in Him.

Our lives are short and fragmentary,
Escape is His through tributary.

Sermons

Many students of the Holy Bible agree on the following:

There is nothing left to be fulfilled on God's prophetic calendar as set forth in Bible before the event which has been called "The Rapture".

This event is foretold in many places, none better than in the apostle Paul's letters to the churches at Corinth and Thessalonica.

1 Corinthians 15: 50-53 KJV
50) "Now I say this brethren, that flesh and blood cannot inherit the kingdom of God: neither doth corruption inherit incorruption.
51) Behold, I show you a mystery; We shall not all sleep, but we shall be changed,
52) In a moment, in the twinkling of an eye, at the last trump: for the trumpet shall sound, and the dead shall be raised incorruptible, and we shall be changed.
53) For this corruptible must put on incorruption, and this mortal must put on immortality."

1 Thessalonians 4: 13-18 KJV
13) "But I do not want you to be ignorant, brethren, concerning those who have fallen asleep lest you sorrow as others who have no hope.
14) For if we believe that Jesus died and rose again, even so God will bring with Him those who sleep in Jesus.

15) For this we say to you by word of the Lord, that we who are alive and remain until the coming of the Lord will by no means precede those who are asleep.

16) For the Lord Himself will descend from heaven with a shout, with the voice of an archangel, and with the trumpet of God. And the dead in Christ will rise first.

17) Then we who are alive and remain shall be caught up together with them in the clouds to meet the Lord in the air. And thus we shall always be with the Lord.

18) Therefore comfort one another with these words.

These two sets of verses only apply to those that are "in Christ", those that have accepted and announced Jesus as Savior and Lord of their lives. Anyone not in that group, called "the Body of Christ" will not be taken. These will be "left behind" and suffer the wrath of God as it is poured out in judgment on a non-believing, sinful world.

It is for this group, these that number themselves "non-believers" and are destined to be "left behind" when Jesus comes again to receive His church unto Himself, that I do what I do...why I preach what I preach...why I bear witness to the truth of God...why I raise up the name of Jesus above all names.

Consider today the words and wisdom in the following sermons. These represent the Word of God as found in the Holy Bible...His inspired word.

Forty different authors, sixty-six books written over a period of fifteen hundred years concluding in the first century AD.

Now matter who you are, no matter what you've done, no matter where you are in life, God, through His beloved son, Jesus Christ want to be invited into your life and have an intimate relationship with you.

Take Him at His word. He loved you so much he gave His life for you that you may know eternal life with Him in the heavens.

I am praying that each of you, as you read the sermons in this collection, will hear the voice of God, that still, small voice, speaking to your heart and mind.

The Samaritan woman at the well, after encountering Jesus, went back to her village saying "Come and see, come and see!"

I can't say it any better or with more power...
Come and see...come and see!

The Power and Message of the Cross

1 Corinthians 1:18 and following

(1:18) For the message of the cross **is foolishness** to those who are perishing, but to us who are being saved it is the power of God.
(19) For it is written (Isaiah, Chapter 29): "I will destroy the wisdom of the wise, and bring to nothing the understanding of the prudent."
(20) Where is the wise? Where is the scribe? Where is the debater of this age? Has not God made foolish the wisdom of this world?
(21) For since, in the wisdom of God, **the world through wisdom did not know God**, it pleased God **through the foolishness** of the message preached to save those who believed.
(22) For Jews request a sign, and Greeks seek wisdom;
(23) but we preach Christ crucified, to the Jews a stumbling block and to the Greeks foolishness,
(24) but to those who are called, both Jews and Greeks, **Christ is the power of God and the wisdom of God.**
(25) Because the foolishness of God is wiser than men, and the weakness of God is stronger than men.

Today's message is not to inform you of something that you do not know, but to remind us all, you and me, of something we should never forget.

To us, **the cross represents God's total revelation** of the gospel message in it's entirety. That in the person of Jesus Christ, is a person who embodies in the flesh, **all** that is God and **all** that is man.

And through His life, death, and resurrection, the entire divine plan and provision **for the redemption of sinful man** is revealed.

Make no mistake, **every single person** who has ever or will ever live is in the process of salvation or destruction by this news…and your response to the cross of Christ determines which.

To the Christ-rejecters, **who are in the process of being destroyed**, the gospel message is nonsense. To those who are believers it is powerful wisdom.

Islam, which now boasts twenty percent of the world's population,

rejects the cross. The Koran says you shall eat of the fruit of your own deeds…therefore, they have no need of a cross.

Humanism, and closely followed by **liberalism** proclaims that we as a species are all capable of evolving into a self-sufficient Jesus of the "Sermon on the Mount" kind. That He himself was actually the example of what we all may become in our ever-evolving enlightenment journey…again, rejecting the cross…and any **need** to be saved.

Truthfully, the cross and it's call to repentance message is trivialized by many evangelicals today. Many point to the apostle Paul's manner of preaching and say, "Well he was preaching that way because that is what was accepted and expected back in those ancient times."

Nothing is further from the truth. Paul's messages were never tailored to the masses, nor tickled their ears.

Firstly, he repelled the Jews as he taught **Christ as the Messiah**, because this was a stumbling block to them. They were looking for a conquering hero to overthrow the Romans and free them from bondage.

And secondly, the Gentiles found the message of a dead and buried carpenters son being some kind of Messiah, to be **utter foolishness**.

To those given eyes to see, **God's power is seen in the weakness of a Messiah on a cross**, and **His wisdom is revealed** in the foolishness of what is preached…that the cross is simply not a central event of biblical theology…but **the** central event of human history.

Imagine requesting to present a lecture today, in any history department in any major university, whereby you would be explaining that no study of ancient times, especially of ancient Roman or Greek culture, would be complete without the bible.

And that they would never be able to understand the bible in question without coming to the knowledge that the cross is God making Himself known to all mankind.

How far do you think you would get in accomplishing this task?

Where could you find a higher education intellectual who would agree that the major problems of this world and the troubles of human life can find their ultimate solution in the execution of an innocent man in AD33?

It is more than obvious that the world, for two thousand years and counting, believes this to be folly.

Yet time and time again, **we see the great apostle preaching Christ crucified**…and we follow in his footsteps and preach this simple message today at Sharon Baptist…that there is **no other name under heaven by which a man may be saved**.

And that the **Jesus of history is the Lord of Glory**, and this same man came into the world where He lived and died and rose again to the pleasure of His father in heaven.

The same one who will return one day accompanied by all who believed, and rule the world from Jerusalem.

I would say, if we're going to get run out of the university, we might as well tell them the whole story, beginning to end.

Like Paul, my purpose is to **preach the word of God** as it pertains to the life and death of His son, the Lord Jesus Christ…and preach it in such a way that people would cease trusting in anything else than the work of God in Christ.

And in doing so, their faith might not rest in the wisdom of man, but in the power of God.

The very story of humanity is the story of **man's rebellion** and subsequent alienation from the God who created him. The death of Jesus, and the picture of this given to us in the bible, causes us to reflect upon the fact that it took the death of His perfect son to deal with our sinful life, our brokenness, and our rebellion.

It is at the foot of the cross that we can find the answers to the age old questions…Where did we come from?…What are we?…and where are we going?

This message is especially important to those of today who have been raised to believe we evolved from time, plus matter, plus chance. In this, we are merely a collection of molecules with no ultimate destination. No navigation needed, endlessly bobbing around in the sea of life, with no direction or purpose.

God wisely established **that man could not come to know Him** by human wisdom. That would exalt man and do nothing to establish the holiness of God.

So God designed a plan to save helpless sinners through the **preaching of a message** that was so simple the worldly "wise" would deem it nonsense.

This alone was the message that Paul would preach because it alone had the power to save all who believed.

The message of the cross, deemed so pointless and irrelevant to man's proud, natural mind, actually **exhibits God greatest power**, His greatest wisdom, and His saving grace abounding in love, for all.

The undeniable generosity of God, the unimaginable sacrifice of Jesus, the unending prompting by God's Holy Spirit all on display in one place for those who believe...

"On a hill far away stood an old rugged cross,
The emblem of suffering and shame,
And I love that old cross where the dearest and best,
For a world of lost sinners was slain"

Amen.
Sources: Alistair Begg "Truth For Life" radio broadcast
        John MacArthur Study Bible
        "The Old Rugged Cross" by George Bennard

A Study of the Book of Colossians

The book of **Colossians** is named for the city of Colossae where the church of Christ was located. This is in ancient Asia Minor, in what is now modern Turkey. It was also to be read in the neighboring church of Laodicea, and yes, that is the same Laodicea that Christ called the "lukewarm church" in **Revelation, Chapter 3**.

The apostle Paul was in prison in Rome when he wrote this letter to the fledgling congregation of believers in Colossae.

The book of Colossians is by Paul's measure, one of his shorter letters, broken down into only four chapters and ninety-five verses. You can read this particular study of the bible in about ten minutes and I encourage you to do so as we unwrap the meaning and application of it's message.

As far as we know, the great apostle never visited Colossae, and the church there was likely founded by one of his converts from his three year ministry in Ephesus, who traveled back home to spread the "good news".

In this case, maybe the unsung hero, Epaphras, mentioned in chapter one.

A decade later, while Paul was under house arrest in Rome, Epaphras tracked him down and pleaded for his help. His church was under attack by popular but destructive teachings that had wormed their way into the congregation...and...as a result, these teachings were weakening the church and its core beliefs in the gospel message.

Paul responds to this request with this letter.
The reader needs to be reminded that ancient Asia Minor was a hostile environment to the early Christian movement. **They faced Eastern philosophy, Hinduism, Buddhism and the like, Jewish legalism concerning the law, pagan astrology and idol worship, mysticism, where one could blend one's consciousness into the consciousness of the Diety through contemplation and self-surrender (think New age occult) and warped Christianity, most formally Gnosticism.**

Gnostics claimed to have access to hidden truths and had special knowledge of so-called "secrets" of the Godhead. They were the spiritually elite and looked down on anyone who were not yet so enlightened.

Into this melting pot caldron of religion comes the Christian convert with his **simple message** "Jesus Saves".

I don't know about you, but those last few paragraphs sound like they were taken from yesterday's news reports rather than describing the world in the first century AD.

Paul took on this tsunami of heresy in this little letter to help true believers there deal with this false doctrine that surrounded them.

Because of this, Colossians today stands on it's own when our core Christian beliefs are under attack.

In his new book, "Christ Above All" Dr. David Jeremiah explains:

"In Colossians, Paul paints one of the most vivid **portraits of Jesus Christ in all of scripture** in order to help believers understand that Christ is above all and superior to any belief system promoted by false voices."

"In Colossians, we see our Lord in His infinite glory.
We see Him shedding this glory to plunge into human history.
We see Him give his life to save humanity and feel the earthquake of His resurrection and ascension to the throne.
And finally we see Him **seated at the right hand of God** with angels, and powers, and dominions subject to Him." (paraphrased)

"The Jesus of Colossians is alive, victorious, and supreme. He is enthroned as supreme Commander in all of heaven, and His return is imminent."

In this short, handcrafted letter by the great apostle you'll find the darkness destroying truth about the "King of Kings and Lord of Lords" and be blessed by every chapter. In this work, Paul proclaims that **Christ is indeed, the fullness of God**.

As in most of Paul's letters, he begins with doctrinal expository in chapters one and two, and finishes with practical application in chapters three and four. We will give preference to the doctrinal chapters and look at them verse by verse.

After introducing himself as the author, he addresses the letter to "the faithful brethren in Christ who are in Colossae". Four times in Colossians, Paul uses the word "faithful" to describe those to whom he is writing.

Adrian Rogers once wrote, "**Faithfulness does not mean we will be perfect**, for there was none perfect but Christ.

We will struggle, we will make poor decisions, we will even occasionally grieve the Holy Spirit with these poor decisions.

But if we are "faithful", **we will continue to trust in God** and do our level best to follow His commandments, even when life is difficult… for we know that nothing can separate us from His love."

As he extends the grace and peace of God, we will pick up the conversation in verse three:

3) "We give thanks to the God and Father of our Lord Jesus Christ, praying always for you,

Here, he affirms that Christ is one with God the Father which establishes His claim to deity.

4) since we first heard of your faith in Christ Jesus and of your love for all the saints;

As we know, love for one another is the visible fruit of all Christians.

5) because of the hope which is laid up for you in heaven, of which you heard before in the word of the truth of the gospel,

The believer's hope is inseparable from his faith. The gospel is the "good news" of Christ's victory over Satan, sin, and death.

6) which has come to you, as it has also in all the world, and is bringing forth fruit, as it is also among you since the day you heard and knew the grace of God in truth;

The gospel was never intended for one special group, it is good news for the world.

7) as you learned from Epaphras, our dear fellow servant, who is a faithful minister of Christ on your behalf,
8) who also declared to us your love in the Spirit."
9) For this reason we also, since the day we heard it, do not cease to pray for you, and to ask that you may be filled with the knowledge of His will in all wisdom and understanding;

A deep and thorough knowledge of the will of God that is finally and completely revealed in the Word of God.

10) that you may walk worthy of the Lord, fully pleasing Him, being fruitful in every good work and increasing in the knowledge of God;

We are called to live in a way that is consistent with the life of the Lord who saved us.

11) strengthened with all might, according to His glorious power, for all patience and longsuffering with joy;

Strengthened that we might endure the trials that come our way.

12) giving thanks to the Father who has qualified us to be partakers of the inheritance of the saints of light.

The Father qualifies or authorizes us through the finished work of the Savior. Apart from God's grace through Christ, the only thing anyone would qualify for would be His wrath.

13) He has delivered us from the power of darkness and conveyed us into the kingdom of the Son of His love,

He has rescued us from Satan's kingdom, the realm of darkness, and brought us into the realm of light with truth and purity. We are then delivered as a gift to His Son.

14) in whom we have redemption through His blood, the forgiveness of sins.

Redemption means to be "delivered by payment of ransom"... most often used in ancient times concerning the freeing of slaves from bondage.

The price of our ransom was the **atoning sacrifice** of His precious blood.

15) He is the image of the invisible God, the firstborn over all creation.

The Greek work for image means "copy" or "likeness". **Jesus Christ is the perfect image--the exact likeness-- of God and is in the very form of God** …and has been so for all of eternity. He is therefore both the representation and manifestation of God. Being the "firstborn", **He outranks all of creation**. He existed before the creation and is exalted in rank above it.

16) For **by Him all things were created** that are in the heavens, and are on the earth, visible and invisible, whether thrones or dominions or principalities or powers. All things were created through Him and by Him.

Many false teachers of the day worshipped angels and included Christ in that group. Paul rejects that and makes it clear that Christ created all things, all things material and all things spiritual, even the holy and fallen angels.

This shows the **immeasurable superiority of Christ** over any being the false teachers should suggest.

17) And He is **before all things** and **in Him all things consist**.

When the universe had it's beginning, Christ already existed…and it is He **who holds it all together now.**

18) And He is the head of the body, the church, who is the beginning, the firstborn of the dead, that in all things He may have preeminence.

Just as the human body is controlled from the brain, **so Christ controls every part of the church** and gives it life and direction. The church had its origin in Christ and His sacrificial death, of which, he was also the first to be resurrected, never to die again. Christ reigns supreme over all who have ever been (or will ever be) resurrected.

19) For it pleased the Father that in Him **all the fullness should dwell**

The Colossian false teachers believed that there was a higher, secret knowledge above the Scriptures that was necessary for enlightenment and salvation. **Here Paul counters that by asserting that in Christ, and Christ alone, is all of the fullness of God**---all the divine powers and attributes are His and not spread among other created beings.

20) and by Him to reconcile all things to Himself, by Him, whether things on earth or things in heaven, having made peace through the blood of His cross.

The Greek word for reconcile means "to change", or "exchange". **Man is only reconciled with God when God restores the relationship** of man with Him through Jesus Christ. This not only concerns man's relationship with God, but through Christ **all** of creation is restored.

21) And you who once were alienated and enemies in your minds by wicked works, yet now He has reconciled
22) in the body of His flesh through death to present you holy and blameless, and above reproach in His sight---
23) if indeed you continue in the faith, grounded and steadfast, and are not moved away from the hope of the gospel which you heard, which was preached to every creature under heaven, of which I, Paul, became a minister.

No matter who you are, before you were reconciled to God through Christ, **you were alienated**, which means "estranged", "cut off", or "separated". In fact there was alienation on both sides. **Non-believers hate the things of God because they love their "wicked works' and God hates their non-repentant sin.**

Because of the believer's union with Christ in His death and resurrection, God considers Christians as Holy as His son. This is the act of **justification**, where we are set apart from our sin and given imputed righteousness.

And those that have been reconciled persevere in the faith and new-found obedience because in addition to being declared righteous, they are actually now **new creations**.

24) I now rejoice in my sufferings for you, and fill up my flesh what is lacking in the afflictions of Christ, for the sake of His body, which is the church.

Despite His death on the cross, Christ's enemies now turned their attention on His disciples, and looked for a new pound of flesh.

Paul willingly endured this persecution to benefit and build up Christ's church.

25) of which I became a minister according to the stewardship from God which was given to me for you, to fulfill the Word of God

A steward was a slave who was put in charge of his master's household, and managed many affairs that were assigned to him by the master. **Paul viewed his ministry as a stewardship from the Lord.**

26) the mystery which has been hidden from ages and from generations, but now has been revealed to His saints.

Many mysteries (or truths of God) were revealed for the first time to the saints of the New Testament.

27) to them God willed to make known what are the riches of the glory of this mystery among the Gentiles: which is Christ in you, the hope of glory.

This is the mystery Paul is referring to: That not only would the Gentiles be welcomed into salvation by the coming Messiah, but that He would **live in the** redeemed church, consisting mostly of Gentiles.

It is this indwelling Spirit of Christ that is the guarantee to each believer of future glory.

28) Him we preach, warning every man and teaching every man in all wisdom, that we may present every man perfect in Christ Jesus.
29) To this end I also labor, striving according to His working which works in me mightily.

The Greek word for striving is "agonizing" which refers to the amount of effort Paul was putting into his work for the Lord, while also acknowledging that it was all being done by God through him.

Chapter Two

1) For I want you to know what a great struggle I have for you and those in Laodicea, and for as many as have not seen my face in the flesh,

Paul struggled mightily to bring the Colossians and Laodiceans to spiritual maturity.

2) that their hearts may be encouraged, being knit together in love and attaining to all riches of the full assurance of understanding, to the knowledge of the mystery of God, both of the Father and of Christ,

A good understanding of the gospel and a shared love for one another are the qualities of mature believers who therefore enjoy the assurance of salvation.

3) in whom are hidden all the treasures of wisdom and knowledge.

Paul is declaring that all the richness of truth---salvation, sanctification, and future glorification---is found in Christ Jesus, who Himself, is God revealed. This statement was most assuredly in the face of the Gnostics who claimed to have "Special Knowledge" only for the spiritually elite.

4) Now this I say lest anyone deceive you with persuasive words.

5) For though I am absent in the flesh, yet I am with you in spirit, rejoicing to see your good order and the steadfastness of your faith in Christ.

Throughout this letter, Paul reaffirms that **everything the believer needs for salvation and spiritual maturity is in Christ**. He did not want to see the rhetoric of the false teachers lead them astray.

And although he could not see them in person, their good order and steadfastness in Christ gave him great joy.

6) As you therefore have received Christ Jesus the Lord, so walk in Him,

7) rooted and built up in Him and established in the faith, as you have been taught, abounding in it with thanksgiving.

"Walk" is a familiar New testament term. **To walk in Christ is to live a life patterned after His**.

Spiritual maturity begins with good roots and a solid foundation in the teachings of the apostles (the books of the New Testament) and is built up from there.

8) Beware lest anyone cheat you through philosophy and empty deceit, according to the tradition of men, according to the basic principles of the world, and not according to Christ.

9) For in Him dwells all the fullness of the Godhead bodily;

10) and you are complete in Him, who is the head of all principality and power.

"Cheat" in the Greek is the same term as robbery. False teachers who are successful in pulling in the untrained, rob them of the truth, their salvation and blessings. "Philosophy" of "the love of wisdom" refers to any theory about God that circumvents the saving grace of Jesus.

Paul calls it "empty deceit"; or worthless deception. False teachers teach "basic principles of the world",

Simplistic, empty, and immature…all inventions of a fallen human system.

Greek philosophy taught that matter was evil and spirit was good, so it was unthinkable that God would ever become man. Paul refutes that by teaching Christ risen…fully God…and fully man.

Believers are complete in Christ who is the creator and ruler of the universe and all its spiritual beings.

11) In Him you were also circumcised with the circumcision made without hands, by putting off the body of the sins of the flesh, by the circumcision of Christ,
12) buried with Him in baptism, in which you also were raised with Him through faith in the working of God, who raised Him from the dead.
13) And you, being dead in your trespasses and the uncircumcision of your flesh, He has made alive together in Him, having forgiven you all trespasses,
14) having wiped out the handwriting of requirements that was against us, which was contrary to us. And He has taken it out of the way, having nailed it to the cross.
15) having disarmed principalities and powers, He made public spectacle of them, triumphing over them in it.

In the Old testament, circumcision symbolized man's need for the cleansing of his fallen heart, and was the outward sign of that cleansing by faith in God.

Here, Paul uses that imagery to describe the believers salvation journey, as they undergo a spiritual "circumcision" at the moment of salvation "by putting off the body of sins of the flesh".

This is the new birth, the new creation in conversion, followed by the outward affirmation of the already inner transformation which is the believers baptism by water.

Where we were once dead in our trespasses, we have been made alive again by the grace of God who nailed these very same trespasses (the handwriting of requirements against us) to the cross along with His cherished son.

The believers sins were all put to Christ's account, then nailed to the cross where He paid the penalty in their place for them all. This act satisfied the wrath of God against crimes that required punishment, not forgiveness.

16) so let no one judge you in food or in drink, or regarding a festival or a new moon or Sabbaths
17) which are a shadow of things to come, but the substance of Christ.
18) Let no one cheat you of your reward, taking delight in false humility and worship of angels, intruding into those things which he has not seen, vainly puffed up by his fleshly mind,
19) and not holding fast to the Head, from whom all the body, nourished and knit together by joints and ligaments, grows with increase that is from God.

In **verses 16-19**, Paul warns the Colossians against trading their new-found freedom in Christ for any set of useless, man-made rules and regulations. Legalism cannot restrain the will to sin, nor eliminate it.

Paul knew and understood the false teachers game. Their go-to move was sleight-of-hand much like the illusionists of today. They coveted the weak-minded and the scripturally ignorant. If they were simply able to begin making you question the reality of a fully man, fully God Christ, they knew that pay dirt could not be far behind.

Interestingly enough, similar false teachers, following the same playbook, running the same scams, are thriving today and deceiving many.

Paul counters this heresy in all of his letters reminding the believers of several key points concerning our relationship with Christ.

Paul asks this question over and over and over again…**You know and acknowledge Jesus as your Savior…but do you also know and acknowledge Him as Lord of your life?**

Put another way…Accepting the free gift of salvation, being cleansed of your sins, and anticipating eternal life in heaven at life's end is at the top of every believers must-do list, but are you also as excited about serving Christ as Lord of your daily life, being obedient to His word and bearing fruit for the kingdom.

Paul points out continuously that these two points must go hand-in-hand.

As Dr. David Jeremiah states in his book, *Christ Above All*, "Everyday, our Lord is working in our lives to make us more like Himself. His desire is our discipleship; His goal is our godliness."

This is what it means to be in Christ…and that is, having Christ **in** us!

Paul preached the saving grace of Christ to the lost sinners of the day, he also preached holding steadfast to one's commitment to Christ that it not be snatched away.

Our commitment to Christ comes with binding string. We have been given a reward we could never earn that comes with certain expectations from the Savior who gave it.

As believers our job is to evangelize, to edify, to make disciples, and help people grow to spiritual maturity so the cycle begins again.

Any dead fish can swim with the current, it takes a live one to swim against it!

In Christ, you have a new purpose for life and a new perspective of what life should be. We must be ready to serve Him at all costs, bringing our wants, desires, and emotions in line with His. We must be ready to speak out for what we believe and possibly suffer the consequences for these actions.

And we must be ready to "struggle" as Paul puts it, using a Greek term closely tied to the endeavor required in athletic competition.

Fence-sitters are truthfully trespassers. They are not tied to either piece of property that the fence line marks because they are suspended in time and space atop the fence. They may want to help themselves to the benefits of the rich property below them, but in truth, they have no claim to either section.

Such is the same of a life in Christ. You were bought with a price. You are no longer your own. **You** belong to **Him**. In Christ, fences are dividing lines between believers and non-believers. They are **not** bleachers…so get off the fence and get to work.

**The harvest fields are full, but the laborers are few.
Are you willing to serve?**

Without this commitment, without this willingness to roll up your sleeves and get to work, without obedience to His word, you will never know all that the Lord has planned for you and stands-at-the-ready to empower you to do.

This is the essence of Paul's letters to the churches. All written from the bowels of a Roman prison. It was his work, he gleefully took it on, Christ empowered Him to do it, and we are thankful today to be encouraged and motivated by it.

20) Therefore, if you died with Christ from the basic principles of the world, why, as though living in the world, do you subject yourselves to regulations---

21) Do not touch, do not taste, do not handle,

22) which all concern things which perish with the using---according to the commandments and doctrines of men?

23) These things indeed have an appearance of wisdom in self-imposed religion, false humility, and neglect of the body, but are of no value against the indulgence of the flesh.

Chapters Three and Four

1) If then you were raised with Christ, seek those things which are above, where Christ is sitting at the right hand of God.

2) Set your mind on things above, not on things of the earth.

3) For you died and your life is hidden with Christ in God.

4) When Christ who is our life appears, then you also will appear with Him in glory.

As Paul moves into what is now known as **chapter three** of his letter to the Colossians, he shifts from the doctrinal issues of chapters one and two, to the new priorities that should exist in the life…
of those who have been "raised' from death to life through Christ.

In **chapters one and two** he describes our blessings in Christ. As **chapter three** unfolds, he describes what our behaviors in Christ should be.

Beginning with the first word in chapter three…which better translates to the word "since", Paul admonishes the believer to seek the things above, because like our savior, we have shared in His death and resurrection. **This is the spiritual renewal and we are now alive in Him so as to understand His spiritual truths**, realities, blessings and the will of His Father in heaven. These are the privileges and riches of the heavenly kingdom…all of which are at our disposal as our inheritance through Christ.

Verse 1 tells us to "seek" these things above and **verse 2** tells us to "set our mind" or think on these things above. Heaven's mysteries open up before us as we stand in obedience and study the word.

As Dr. Jeremiah says, "in the first century, people only had to look at Jesus to see what God is like. In the twenty-first century, people should only have to look at us to see what Jesus is like."

Verse 3 tells us we are "hidden in Christ" which implies security. We are therefore protected, no matter how the world may rage against us, and our own circumstances crumble, our innermost spirit is safe and secure, hidden with Christ in God. We have spiritual resources to sustain us in Christ that the world can't see.

No matter what happens in this life we must never forget...Jesus, the son of God is risen and sits at the right hand of the Father...and when we see Him next He will be revealed in all His glory and magnificence... just as we will be transformed to be like Him!

What? How?...**verse 4**..."When Christ who is our life appears, then you will also appear with Him in glory."

It is important to note this truth, as noted by Paul in this letter:

Jesus Christ is not only the Creator, "for by Him were all things created" Colossians 1:16...but He will return again one day to **receive** all things unto Himself, to the glory of God the Father.

The book of Revelation describes in detail the horrors of the last days of earth as the wrath of God is poured out on a non-believing, fallen world, but it also describes the triumphant return of the King of Kings, Jesus Christ to **reclaim** what is His.

As Head over the church, He has reconciled all things to Himself through His death on the cross and has redeemed believers, making them spotless before God.

Paul reminds us of our "practical application" of this knowledge.

Since we have died to ourselves in Christ, we have also been raised with Him and should live a life of submission to His will.

If indeed, He is **"Lord over all"**, the life we live as a Christian should be transformed in every area. Christ, then, provides total and complete sufficiency in our lives…from salvation through sanctification…**Christ provides it all**.

"Do not lie to one another, since you have put off the old man with his deeds," Paul tells us in chapter three, verse 9, "and have put on the new man who is renewed in knowledge, according to the image of Him who created him, where there is neither Greek nor Jew, circumcised nor uncircumcised, barbarian, Scythian, slave not free, **but Christ is all and in all**."

These are the lessons of Paul's letter to the church in Colossae.
May we all be blessed by it's reading and study.
Sources: John MacArthur Study Bible
    Insight for Living Ministries: Colossians
    Dr. David Jeremiah: Christ Above All

Proclaiming the Truth of the Gospel

Various Passages

As we've discovered in our study of the book of Colossians, over the last few weeks, the apostle Paul reminds us that everything we need is to be found in Christ.

He not only is in everything we know, but **He made everything** that exists and one day **will return to take possession** of what He made.

And through **His finished work on the cross**, for those that believe, **there is redemption of sin and eternal life** with Him when He returns in His glory and triumph.

"Since we were **raised with Him**, (become part of His resurrection) says Paul, then we should seek the things that are above, where Christ sits at the right hand of the Father." **Colossians 3:1**

We also learned in our study of the book of **Romans (8:17),** that if we are now children of God, we are also joint heirs with Christ…
and while we may suffer with Him for the sake of the gospel, we may also be glorified with Him.

Because of this, "We need not worry over the things of this world, or it's ideals, because we are hidden with Christ in God." **Colossians 3:3**

But Paul knew other things as well…most importantly, that if he was to be a **light shining into the darkness**, if he was going **to be faithful to the end** and **endure** whatever came his way concerning his calling to preach the gospel of Christ, there had to be some anchors, **some certainties** to carry with him through.

These would be the **immoveable guide posts** in his ministry. These would be **untouchable truths** he would never be persuaded to replace. These beliefs would follow him to the grave, or giving his life for Christ, whichever came first.

He lived for the certainty of the **superiority and exclusivity** of the New Covenant as it had been revealed in Christ, he was certain he had been made a minister of this mercy, and he was certain that he needed to have a pure heart as he went about this work.

In his book, *"Seven Ways to Fix the World"*, author Gordon Brown lists the following: institute global health, insure economic prosperity for all, establish rigid climate change initiatives, access to education for all, raise humanitarianism standards around the world, abolish tax havens for corporations and the rich, and eliminate nuclear weapons.

Also getting votes in Mr. Brown's book, adapting a low-energy lifestyle and putting women in charge of more things…(no mention of Mrs. Betty). When I read this I thought, "I'm 69 years old…I'm already living a low-energy lifestyle!"

Now I'm not sure any of these would have made the apostle Paul's top ten list. Most notably, not a word about Christ in Mr. Brown's summation, which our great apostle would never have agreed with.

Now we know in our studies that the world is made up of two kingdoms, the kingdom of light and the kingdom of darkness…and we are told in **2 Corinthians Chapter 6** that **lightness and darkness are incompatible**. As incompatible as lawlessness and righteousness, as

Satan and Christ, as unbelievers and believers. **Therefore one has no business bonding with the other.**

Therefore the word of God **calls us to be separate**, to touch not the unclean thing, to have no fellowship with unfruitful works of darkness.

The kingdom of light is not ever helped or advanced by an alliance in a common cause with the kingdom of darkness.

Christ does not need Satan to accomplish his purposes…and when we start compromising with false teachers who are not preaching the word of God, this becomes the source of many problems in the church.

Our responsibility is to **shine the light into the darkness**, not try to find common ground with it. We are lights in the world, we have the same calling as the apostle Paul. In **Romans Chapter 1** he says, **14)** "I am under obligation to the Greeks, and to the Barbarians; both to the wise and to the unwise.

15) So, as much as in me, I am ready to preach the gospel to you that are in Rome also.
16) For I am not ashamed of the gospel of Christ: for it is the power of God unto salvation to every one that believes; to the Jew first, and also to the Greek.

Paul never backed up from preaching the gospel of Christ.
He is an example of how we should be found shining our light into the darkness…and the only way he could continually be this example, in the face of all the trials that came his way, was to have **unchangeable beliefs** in his message and his calling.

The undeniable truth is that many around you **are on their way to destruction**. The question before us is, "Do you care enough to shine your light into their darkness?"

Do you understand **they have no hope without it?**

The great apostle understood this well and was willing to commit his life, even lay down his life, for the gospel of Christ. This certainty in his message kept him bold and committed until he was martyred.

He never lost the wonder over the fact that he was called to do something that he didn't deserve to do. He was not worthy to carry this message. Not at all…and he knew it. That is why he refers to himself as the chief of sinners.

1 Timothy 1:15 "This is a faithful saying and worthy of all acceptance, that **Christ Jesus came into the world to save sinners, of whom I am chief.**"

Yet, Paul would not abandon his ministry. He knew with certainty the gospel of Christ was true, he knew he had been appointed by Christ to preach it, and he trusted God to strengthen him to withstand the trials that would come his way because of his calling.

In the living Bible translation, **2 Corinthians 4, verses 1 and 2**, Paul tells us, "It is God himself, in His mercy, who has given us this wonderful work (of telling his Good News to others) and so we never give up. We do not try to trick people into believing---we are not interested in fooling anyone. We never try to get anyone to believe that the Bible teaches what it doesn't. All such shameful methods we forego. We stand in the presence of God, and as we speak, we tell the truth, as all who know us will agree."

And then in **verse 5**, "We don't go around preaching about ourselves, **but about Christ Jesus as Lord**. All we say of ourselves is that we are your slaves because of what Jesus has done for us."

When was the last time you thought of yourself as a slave, bound to the redemption that Christ has so freely provided you?

Again in the Living Bible, **1 Corinthians, chapter six, verses 19-20**, Paul tells us, "Haven't you yet learned that **your body is the home of the Holy Spirit God gave you** and that He lives in you? Your own body does not belong to you. For God has bought it with a great price. So use every part of your body to give glory back to God, because He owns it."

And in **1 Thessalonians 2:4** "But as we have been approved by God to be entrusted with the gospel, even so we speak, not as pleasing men, but God who examines our heart."

This is the essence of the gospel message and the best possible truth for all Christians to hear…that if you will simply proclaim the truth of Christ, it will **commend** itself to the heart of the hearer. No craftiness, no deceptiveness, no adding to or taking away…just declare the truth. The truth of sin, the penalty thereof, and the **release from that sin debt by the shed blood of Christ at Calgary.**

Paul was certain that salvation and the redemption of sin was the sovereign work of God…and if this message was truthfully and honorably preached…it, on its own, would **commend** (cause to be acceptable or pleasing) itself to the heart of the hearer.

Salvation is the light of Christ shining in the darkened heart. It is creation…something that is there where there was nothing before.

That's why **2 Corinthians 5:17** says, "Therefore if anyone is in Christ, he is a **new creation**; old things have passed away; behold all things have become new."

Non-believers, of which we once were, **are saved by grace, and that not even of yourselves, lest any man should boast.**

God gives you the gift of repentance and faith because He wills to give you life. Not only abundant, joyful life in this life, but continuing on into eternity with Him.

So what do we do? We preach not ourselves. **We preach Jesus Christ** as Lord of Lords and King of Kings!

And when we do, the riches of our Heavenly Father are showered down upon us!

The gains far outweigh the cost!

Amen.

What to do With the Time "In-Between"

Various Passages

Everyone in America knows what to do with the time in-between the ages of 5 and 18...you go to school and get an education... kindergarten first, then grades 1-12.

There is also little doubt that those who diligently follow this path, take it seriously, study and work hard, will exit the program with the best chance of moving on to even higher levels of education and doing well in the game of life.

The apostle Paul, who's work in the New Testament we have been studying lately, was first and foremost a scholar. He knew well the benefits of committing oneself to a subject, learning it backwards and forwards, and then putting this knowledge to use in his daily life.

Paul's conversion on the road to Damascus, changed his life and as he states in **2 Corinthians 5:17**, "Therefore, if any man be in Christ, he is a new creation; old things have passed away; behold all things are new."

However, the Paul who wrote these and many other wonderful statements, is not the same Paul that was converted on the road to Damascus.

Paul was **converted to Christianity in 33 AD** after Jesus was crucified, resurrected, and ascended to heaven. He was **martyred in Rome for preaching the gospel in 62-64 AD.**

One of the books he wrote during this time (which we just quoted) was **2 Corinthians**, which was penned in 55AD.

The title of today's message is *"What to do With the Time In-Between".* The real question that it asks is "What are **you** doing with the time between **your** conversion into Christ and the day He calls you home at life's end?"

Now few of us have the benefit of receiving the gospel directly from Jesus as Paul claims in the first chapter of **Galatians**. Nor have any of us spent three years in the desert sorting through the things we had been taught.

What we do have is a wealth of information at our fingertips called the Holy Bible, we also have the internet to help break down troublesome passages, and we have the Holy Spirit alive and well inside us all to direct us in our quest for spiritual knowledge.

In addition to this one could add Christian radio and TV broadcast stations that are full of biblical teaching.

The Bible records what Paul did with his "in-between" time from his conversion to martyrdom.

Again, what are you doing with yours?

Our "in-between" living can be gut wrenching, heart crushing, and faith challenging…but it can also be **freedom in it's purest form,**

and absolutely exhilarating as we interact with our maker in a personal relationship day after day. This is the time between our justification and future glorification.

In a recent radio broadcast of "Grace to You", John MacArthur was doing a question and answer session with his church. In one of his answers, he acknowledged that if he had to pick, he would choose **2 Corinthians** as his favorite book in the New Testament.

This book explores the relationship between Paul and the church at Corinth as he agonizes over some of the things that are going on there.

For John MacArthur it "represents the agonies of disappointment and the agonies of failures and success in the life of any given church"…as seen by the pastor.

Let's look together at **2 Corinthians 4, verse 13 and following** (from The Living Bible):

13) "We boldly say that we believe (trusting God to care for us), just as the Psalm writer did when he said, **"I believe and therefore I speak"**.

14) We know that the same God who brought the Lord Jesus back from death **will also bring us back to life again** with Jesus, and present us to Him along with you.

15) These sufferings of ours are for your benefit. And the more of you who are won to Christ, the more there are to thank Him for His great kindness, and the more the Lord is glorified.

16) That is why I never give up. Though our bodies are dying, our inner strength in the Lord is growing every day.

17) These troubles and sufferings of ours are, after all, **quite small and won't last very long**. Yet this short time of distress will result in God's richest blessing upon us forever and ever!

18) So we do not look at what we can see right now, the troubles all around us, but we **look forward to the joys in heaven** which we have not seen.

The troubles will soon be over, but the joys to come will last forever.

"I believe and therefore I speak". This is our calling, this is our purpose, this is how we honor God's guiding hand in our life.

In **2 Timothy**, as he writes to the young pastor, Paul gives him one command: "Preach the Word of God urgently at all times, whenever you get the chance, in season and out, when it is convenient and when it is not." **2 Timothy 4:2**

(The Living Bible).

Our God is **fully present and fully engaged** as you transverse this time of "in-between". As Hagar, the hand maid of Sarah came to know as she wandered in the wilderness, **our God is the God who "sees"**. He "sees" us in every trial, every victory, every test…and it is this activity in our lives that gives us hope for what is to come.

We are **all** unworthy of the grace we have received. We are **all** unworthy of the calling we have been given.

The great apostle says that if you are looking for a good place to start, **start with a pure heart**.

He says, "My conscience is clear, I have lived with a clear conscience." Set your eyes on things above, rather that the things of this world (which we learned last week).

This is winning the spiritual battle in the heart so that you don't live with an **accusing conscience**…that will suck the life out of anyone. This can only be achieved by living a life of discipline. This requires taking control of every aspect of your life…up to and including your thought life and what comes out of your mouth.

Jesus Himself said, "It is not **what goes into the mouth** of a man that defiles and dishonors him, but **what comes out of the mouth** that defiles and dishonors him." **Matthew 15:11**

Paul longed not only to serve his risen Lord, he longed to be with Him. In his letter to the Philippians, we read, **"For me, living is Christ, but**

should I die, I would consider that gain…but if living for Him and preaching His message gives me more opportunities to win others to the kingdom, I don't know which is better, to live or to die!"

I long to go and be with Him! How much happier for me than being here!

But the fact is I can still be **useful to Him down here**, so here I stay helping you grow and become happy in your faith.

Philippians 1: 21-26 paraphrased

These are marching orders for us all, for we know we are here for only a little while…as the Bible tells us…**"like a mist that appears and then vanishes"**. And while we (especially those of us up in years like Miss Betty) may be ready for the Lord to call us home, there is still much work to be done here.

Jesus himself told His disciples, **"The harvest truly is plentiful, but the laborers are few**. Therefore pray the Lord of the harvest to send out laborers into His harvest." **Matthew 9: 37-38**

Our Father can't pour out His riches **into hands that are already full**. Matthew tells us, "No one can serve two masters; for either he will hate the one and love the other, or else he will be loyal to the one and despise the other. You cannot serve God and mammon" (which is defined as earthly, material treasures…especially money). **Matthew 6: 24**

The Pharisees (and today, the world) taught that devotion to God and devotion to money were perfectly compatible.

This complemented the commonly-held notion **that earthly riches signified divine blessing**. Christ denounced the love of money and the devotion to earthly treasures. He knew the distraction it could become in the life of a believer and was an idol in the making.

The apostle Paul, not one to shy away from any subject, addresses this in his first letter to Timothy. "But those who desire to be rich **fall into temptation and a snare**, and into many foolish and harmful lusts which drown men in destruction and perdition. **For the love of money is the root of all kinds of evil**, for which some have strayed from the faith in their greediness, and pierced themselves through with many sorrows." **1 Timothy 6: 9-10**

The key word here is **"love"**. It doesn't say the accumulation of money, nor the use of money…but the love of money which speaks of putting it first in your life ahead of God.

Lastly, I will ask you again…how are your spending your in-between time as we await the return of our Lord Jesus, or being called to heaven at life's end, whichever comes first?

This question is due your immediate attention because the **hour is late and our time is short.**

The Fig Tree and The Money-Changers

Mark 11: 12-25

When you leave here today and arrive back home, the chances are that you will turn on a light or two, maybe heat up lunch on the stove, watch an NFL game, or even decide to vacuum the living room.

All of these things require one thing...**electricity**.

Which in turn requires another thing, and that is, **permission or authority provided to you by the power company** to use their electricity. Without that, you can click the switch all you want and nothing will happen.

Christ gave His disciples a good lesson in how things get done in the kingdom of God in **Mark Chapter 11**. If you have your Bibles, turn to verse 12 and following:

12) "Now the next day, when they had come out of Bethany, He was hungry.
13) And seeing from afar a fig tree having leaves, He went to see if perhaps He would find something on it. When He came to it, He found nothing but leaves, for it was not the season for figs.
14) In response Jesus said to it, "Let no one eat fruit from you ever again."
And his disciples heard it.

15) So they came to Jerusalem. Then Jesus went into the temple and began to drive out those who bought and sold in the temple, and overturned the tables of the money changers and the seats of those who sold doves.

16) and he would not allow anyone to carry wares through the temple.

17) Then He taught, saying to them, "Is it not written, 'My house shall be called a house of prayer for all nations'? But you have made it a den of thieves.

18) And the scribes and chief priests heard it and sought how they might destroy Him; for they feared Him, because all the people were astonished at His teaching.

19) When evening had come, He went out of the city.

20) Now in the morning, as they passed by, they saw the fig tree dried up from the roots.

21) And Peter, remembering, said to Him, "Rabbi, look! The fig tree which You cursed has withered away."

22) So Jesus answered and said to them "Have faith in God.

23) For assuredly I say to you, whoever says to this mountain, 'Be removed and be cast into the sea, and does not doubt in his heart, but believes that those things he says will be done, he will have whatever he says.

24) Therefore I say to you, whatever things you ask when you pray, believe that you will receive them and you will have them.

On the face of it, in these passages, we see what could be construed as **two completely different teaching moments, by Christ with his disciples.**

One must always keep in mind the timeline of this week (which was Passover) and that Jesus **knew the cross awaited Him** at week's end. Here, and within the few days left, was all the time He would have with them before that horrific event.

So these last few days needed to count as He **prepared to transfer His ministry to them.** Jesus was indeed a power station on His own--authorized and powered by His father in heaven--and He was constantly transferring this power to His disciples.

As we return to the passages with this in mind, we see that Mark has taken one complete story **(the cursing of the fig tree)** divided it in half, and used it to bracket another complete story **(the cleansing of the temple).**

Actually, he has told the two stories as they happened in the timeline. Jesus cursed the fig tree while they were on their way into Jerusalem on Monday morning. He then proceeded to cleanse the temple before venturing back out of the city.

Then, on Tuesday morning as they reentered the city, the disciples noticed the fig tree had withered over night. Interesting enough, Jesus did not stay in Jerusalem overnight, but traveled the short distance to Bethany to stay with Mary, Martha, and Lazarus, who Jesus had raised from the dead.

My Mother was a gardener by hobby. In our yard, as I was growing up were orange trees, pecan trees, persimmon trees, grape vines, and kumquat trees,0 to name just a few.

There were also two very large fig trees. One in the side yard and one just out the back door. So I know well the growing cycle of fruit producing fig trees.

You could expect two crops a year, one in the summer and one in the fall. In between they would look extremely barren with hardly a leaf on them. However, as the producing season was closing in, you would notice large green, healthy leaves...followed by budding fig fruit.

As these would ripen they would change color from green to a dark shade of purple, and finally, fully ripened, would crack open exposing a lighter purple/to reddish interior.

At this time, If you could beat the blue jays to them, you could pick a "mess of figs"…to eat or preserve.

Now on this particular Monday, in Jerusalem many years ago, Jesus was entering the city and saw a fig tree full of leaves. Being hungry, he approached the tree in hopes of finding fruit to eat.

Unfortunately, this tree had yet to produce any fruit as it was still early in the growing season, despite the fact, being full of leaves, **it was representing the fact that it was also, at that time, producing fruit.**

As the disciples watched and heard, Jesus then cursed the tree for it's lack of production and continued on toward the temple.

The temple was the beating heart of the Jewish community. Here was their house of worship and the place to bring animals to sacrifice for the atoning of their sin. It was to be a holy site…a house of prayer, cleansing, and reflection on the wonders of Jehovah God.

What Jesus found instead in the outer courts was an open-air commerce center featuring booth after booth of **entrepreneurs who were skimming money** off of the thousands of religious travelers who were to celebrate Passover. No matter your need of a goat, ram, bull, ox, or even a dove…it could all be provided for you by the market vendors at two or three times the normal price.

"Cash, credit, or debit, sir?"…the only question.

As He witnessed what was going on in the outer courts of His Father's house, in His most holy city of Jerusalem He **became greatly angered** and proceeded to clean out this man-made money-making site post haste.

Single handedly, he waded into them, overturning their tables and physically showing them to the door…not allowing them to take a single thing with them.

"This is my Father's house!…a house of prayer!" he roared, **"and you have turned it into a den of thieves!"**

To the amazement of all gathered, including His disciples who recorded the event in their gospels, Jesus **cleared the temple** and restored it to the house of worship and prayer for which it was designed.

They then returned to Bethany for the night.

On the way back into the city the next day, Tuesday, Peter noticed the fee tree had withered overnight and remarked about it to Jesus.

Jesus answered, **"Have faith in God**. This is where it starts…and whoever has this faith, and does not doubt, but believes, will see his prayers answered when he asks."

I would like to make two points about these passages we have highlighted this morning.

1) The cursing of the fig tree coupled with the cleansing of the temple highlights exactly how our savior feels about fakes.

In the first example, the fig tree was **representing that it was producing fruit, but was not**. In the second example, the vendors in the outer courts were **representing that they were there to be of great help to the incoming worshipers. This was not the case.**
They were there to line their pockets with money while overcharging everyone who passed by.

These examples are still relevant to us today as they can represent the worst of the body of Christ. This would be **Christians who are in many ways pretending to be something they are not**. Our Lord is not looking for place holders. He is searching the earth for **workers**, laborers in the field. The Great Commission was given to the apostles and through them, down to us today.

He has no time, nor favor, **for believers who are representing fruit and producing none. He sees right through you.**

Worse, he **despises anyone** who claims to represent Him and is only in it for personal gain. When He told the disciples to go out into all the word, spreading the word and bringing men to the truth, I don't remember him sending them to the Mercedes dealership first.

Anyone using His name to fleece the public of their money is **headed for judgment** and will one day find out how costly a mistake he has made.

2) "Have faith in God"...a surprising answer in response to the withered tree, yet Jesus, knowing the hour was late, wanted them to see first hand yet another example of operating within the Father's will.

He wanted them to know that through "Faith in God" **all things are possible**. He also knew that when he ascended into heaven, the Holy Spirit would come empowering these same disciples to do "far greater works than He". **John 14:12**

Additionally, He knew the Holy Spirit would **"teach them all things and remind them of all the things Jesus said"** (in their three years together) **John 14:26**

These two teaching moments were followed that night by Jesus sharing with the disciples what would be happening in the world just before His return.

Serious discussions on serious matters. This was passion week, the week our savior went to the cross...which is the **centrality of the gospel message**.

So the next time you flip a light switch, or turn on the stove, or lower the thermostat, be glad for good standing and relationship with your power company.

And the next time you go to the Father in prayer, be thankful for the power you may access through the completed work of our Savior on the cross.

The uncountable riches of heaven are yours if you believe in God without doubt and ask in Jesus name.

Sources: Alistair Begg Radio Broadcast
          Tony Evans Radio Broadcast

The Celebration of Passover, The Significance of Communion, and The "Body" of Christ

Matthew Chapter 26

Passover week (usually the first week in April) is arguably the greatest of all Jewish ceremonial events. It honors the week that Jehovah God dealt a crushing blow to Pharaoh of Egypt.

In the Old testament book of **Exodus**, Moses tells of the many plagues that God caused to fall on Egypt until Pharaoh was persuaded to let His chosen nation Israel, go free. In His last and final plague to spread across the land, God sent an avenging angel to **kill every first born son in the land**. Only by first covering their doorposts **with the blood of a sacrificial lamb** were the captive Jews able to survive this horrible loss of life. Simply put, when the avenging angel of Jehovah God saw the blood on the doorposts, he **"passed over"** the homes of the Israelites, sparing the firstborn children inside.

This ceremonial week is still celebrated and observed around the world today by Jews and Gentiles alike.

For this week also commemorates the same week that **Jesus of Nazareth became the sacrificial lamb** for all mankind, by freely giving His life on the cross, conquering sin, Satan, and death in the process.

"Oh death, where is thy sting? Oh grave, where is thy victory? But thanks be to God, who giveth us the victory through our Lord Jesus Christ." **1 Corinthians 15: 55-57**

This verse is truth because of the **completed work** of Christ on the cross in **33 AD**.

Today we celebrate this historical event in the **taking and receiving** of communion as Christ himself directed his apostles, **"Do this is remembrance of me"** so many years ago.

He established this during what is known as the **Last Supper**…the last meal Jesus shared with all twelve of his disciples prior to his crucifixion.

Imagine if you will, the mind of Christ on this night.

As they reclined around the table to share the meal, Jesus, being fully God and fully man, knew well the events that were about to unfold and the burden he would bear…not just for them…but for all mankind.

He also **knew each one of them completely** and the testing that would come to each of them in the near future. He had just spent **three years pouring himself into them**, preparing them for the hour of His departure, and knowing full well, that despite His best efforts, **they were far from ready**.

As we look around the room through His eyes, we see the **impetuous Peter**, a fisherman by trade, who seemingly had a knack for always saying the wrong thing at the wrong time. Beside Peter, **his brother Andrew**, together since the beginning, when Jesus called them both. Jesus knew **crucifixion awaited them both in the coming years.**

We also see **James and John**, brothers, (who Christ called the **"sons of thunder"** for their enthusiasm), whose mother asked that He would give them positions at His left and right hand when he came into His kingdom.

James would be the first to be martyred for the cause, beheaded by King Herod Agrippa, 22 years later.

Many years later, Christ would visit **John**, the last remaining apostle on the Isle of Patmos, and dictate letters to the seven churches in Asia Minor.

He also commanded him to record the visions he was about to be shown. **This became the book of Revelation.**

Then **Matthew** (the despised former tax collector, who went on to author the first gospel), and **Phillip** (who would go on to preach the gospel in Greece and Syria) **were both later martyred for the gospel.**

Then **Thomas** (who would later demand physical proof before believing that Jesus had indeed been resurrected), and **Bartholomew** (who we know very little about) **both later gave their lives for the preaching of Christ as Savior.**

Then **James**, known as **"James the Less"** (simply to distinguish him from the other James, the brother of John) would later be thrown from the pinnacle of the Temple at Jerusalem for preaching Christ, then stoned and bashed with a club.

And finally, **Judas** the keeper of the money (who would betray Him) committed suicide. **Jude** (a brother of Jesus, who preached Christ crucified and authored the book of Jude) and **Simon the Zealot** (another apostle we know little about) **both gave their lives for Christ in the years to come.**

And there you have it. Not a theologian, not a university professor, not a Mensa member in the room. Twelve young men with no particular talents or attributes other than loving their Rabbi and faithfully following Him over the last three years.

And it was these young men, this group, that He would entrust with the **Great Commission** to "go and make disciples of all nations, baptizing them in the name of the Father and the Son and of the Holy Spirit, and teaching them to obey everything I have commanded you." **Matthew 28: 16-20**

To these he gave this commandment on this night as it is recorded in **Matthew 26:26** and following:

26) And as they were eating, Jesus took the bread, blessed and broke it, and gave it to the disciples and said, "Take, eat, this is My body."

27) Then he took the cup, and gave thanks, and gave it to them saying, "Drink from it, all of you."

28) "For this is My blood of the new covenant, which is shed for many for the remission of sins."

In this way, Jesus transformed Passover into the first observance of what we now call the **"Lord's Supper".** In his crucifixion the next day, He at once became **the sacrificial lamb of Passover** ("The Lamb of God") and the **elements of the communion service** (his broken body represented by the broken loaf of bread and the cup of wine representing His shed blood for a one-time, all-time remission of sin).

By participating in this remembrance of Christ on the cross, **we strengthen our relationship with Him.** Because of Him we now enjoy **victory** instead of **slavery** to sin. No longer is your past an excuse to keep you from being the man or woman God intended you to be. Because you are no longer that person, **you are a new creation in Christ.** We have been **set free from the bondage of sin** and **that freedom came at a high cost to Jesus,** which he willingly paid... following the Father's will, not His own.

In this one act, Jesus has reconciled **God's mercy and love for man** with **His obligation to hand out judgment as the penalty for sin.** Because of this joining of God's **mercy and judgment,** there is now **"no condemnation for those who are in Christ Jesus".** **Roman 8:1**

At the resurrection of Christ, God is announcing that **condemnation had been condemned!**

When the Pharisees brought the woman before Him who had been caught in the act of adultery, He challenged them to throw the first stone if none of them had broken the law of Moses.

When they all dropped their rocks, He told the woman, that He did not condemn her either.

He didn't condemn her, even though it was right and just to do so, because He knew in a very short time **He would be willing to be condemned for her**. Jesus doesn't sweep sin under the rug, **He puts it under His blood**.

Jesus last recorded words to His disciples were: "Ye shall be witnesses unto me both in Jerusalem, and in all Judea, and in Samaria, and to the uttermost part of the earth." **Acts 1:8**

The book of Acts is **the story of the men and women** who took those words seriously and **began to spread the news of a risen savior** to the most remote corners of the known world.

And in **Acts 2: 41-42** we read:
41) "Then they that gladly received his word (in this case Peter) **were baptized**: and the same day there were added unto them about **three thousand souls**.
42) And they continued steadfastly in the **disciples doctrine** and **fellowship, and in the breaking of bread**, and in **prayers**.

So we see in the early foundational days of the church, **these four pillars of the faith** were taught and observed:
1) steadfastly following the gospel doctrine (obedience)
2) continuing in fellowship (supporting, loving, encouraging each other)
3) the breaking of bread (observance/remembrance of communion)
4) praying (as Paul says… "without ceasing")

So this is the importance of **communion** that we reverently observe today.

We **remember the suffering of Christ** as He gave His life freely for ours.

And when we **remember what Jesus Christ did for us**, we embrace the word of God and love Him all the more.

Amen.

Made For Worship

John 4: 20-24

It's more than obvious that **human beings were made for worship**. We can look in every nook and cranny in the world and we will find **human beings worshipping something**.

In some places, it may be **pagan idols and pagan gods**. Maybe we'll even find (as in the days of ancient Rome) **a god for every day of the year.**

Or maybe we will find people **who worship their ancestors** and are continually asking for their guidance and blessings.

There are **astrologers** who actively **worship the sky** and allow the movement of the sun, moon, and stars to rule their lives.

And don't forget the **atheists,** who say **there is no such thing as God**…they too, worship. It may be **themselves**, it may be **money and processions**, and it may be **pleasure and leisure**, but this all is a form of worship.

Finally, there are those of us in the Christian faith, who stand and say **there is a God, and His name is Jehovah**, and as the four living creatures around the throne of God, we sing, **"Holy, holy, holy, is the Lord God Almighty, who was and is and is to come."**

So we can stand here today and say that this **aging, sinful world** in which we live is **full** of worship.

But is it **true worship**, which the Lord our God desires and finds pleasing ...or **is it false worship** leading many down the path of destruction?

Are we getting our directions from **the Word of God**?...or **following the herd** and the movement of the world?

The best place to start is to define exactly what **"true worship"** is.

If you have your bibles, turn to the **4th chapter of John**:

To set the stage, Jesus is involved in a **conversation with a Samaritan woman**. Now this is not the **"Good Samaritan"** you may have read about.

In fact she is **just the opposite**, and as we have already found out in the narrative, she has had **five husbands and is living unmarried with potential husband number six.**

As I'm sure you will agree, this statement alone, colors her as a person of questionable character.

We will pick up the conversation in verse 19:
19) The woman said to Him, "Sir, I perceive you are a prophet.
20) Our fathers worshipped on this mountain, and you Jews say that in Jerusalem is the place where one ought to worship."

To clarify, the Jews, who **recognized the entire Old Testament**, chose **Jerusalem on Mount Zion** as their worship site. The Samaritans, who were actually what you might call half-breeds...half Jew, half Gentile, only **recognized the first five books by Moses**, chose **Mount Gerizim** for their temple of worship, because that was the first place Abraham built an altar to God.

21) Jesus said to her, "Woman believe Me, **the hour is coming** when you will neither on this mountain, nor in Jerusalem, worship the Father."

There was no reason to debate these locations, because Jesus knew that both places would soon be obsolete and would have no part in the lives of those who genuinely worshipped God.

22) "You worship **what you do not know**; **we know what we worship**, for salvation is of the Jews."

The Samaritans did not know God. They did not have the full revelation of Him (the complete Old testament) and therefore could not worship in truth.

The Jews did know the God they worshipped which **was revealed in the Old Testament when salvation first came to them**. Later it would come through them (The Lion of Judea) to the world.

23) "But the hour is coming, **and now is**, when true worshipers will **worship the Father in spirit and in truth**; for the **Father is seeking such to worship Him**."

The "hour" refers to **Jesus' death, burial, resurrection, and ascension to God** having fulfilled the work of redemption.

Jesus was making the point that in light of His coming **as Messiah and Savior**, worshipers will not be identified by a **particular shrine or temple**, but by their **worship of the Father through the Son**.

"True worshipers" then are those everywhere that worship God through the son, **from the heart (in the spirit)**.

24) "**God is Spirit** and those who worship Him **must worship in truth and spirit**."

This phrasing means God is invisible and man could never comprehend Him unless He chooses to reveal Himself to man.

Therefore, we can never know **the depth and length and width of God,** nor in any way can we **begin to fully understand our God** until He **reveals His thoughts, words, and wisdom to us in His holy scripture…**which he has done for **His adopted children under the Son.**

John MacArthur and another noted evangelist were once guests on The Larry King Show.

A half hour of spirited discussion into the program, the noted evangelist continued to use the phrase, **"Well, My Jesus"** as he argued doctrinal points with John. "Well, my Jesus doesn't think like that…Well, my Jesus doesn't judge like that"…and so on and so on…

Finally, John said, "Time Out!…there is no **YOUR** Jesus. There is only **one Jesus, our Jesus,** and that is **the Jesus revealed in scripture.** If you are quoting an **attribute** or **quality** or **sentiment** of Jesus **that isn't founded in revealed scripture,** you stand in error and falsehood."

So the question at hand today is **are you a true worshipper?** Or to put it another way as was recently heard at River Christian Church…**are you a fan or a follower of Jesus?**

Are we offering to God **true worship that is pleasing to Him, that is acceptable to Him?…**because the very reason we are gathered here today is to worship Him.

To help us along, we come away with three discoveries about the nature of worship from this story of the woman at the well:

1) True worship is not about a place.
Many Christians today call their place of worship the **sanctuary.**

A noted theologian of yesteryear refused to allow his congregation to call the worship center where they met a sanctuary.

He said, **"A sanctuary is a holy place. Therefore this room is not a sanctuary. The Christians who meet here are the sanctuaries."**

1 Corinthians 6:19 tells us this: "Or do you not know that your body is the **temple (sanctuary) (holy place)** of the Holy Spirit who is in you, whom you have from God and you are not your own? **For you were bought with a price**, therefore glorify God in your body, and in your spirit which are God's."

Our God doesn't live here in this house, he lives here in your heart.

2) True worship is not about a performance.
It's not about checking in, checking boxes and going home.

Did I come to Sunday school today?…check. **Did I stay for church?…** check. **Did I drop a few dollars in the plate?…**check. **Did I stay awake for the entire message?….**ok, for most of it…check.

That's what the **Pharisees** did. They checked all the boxes, then wanted to raise that up to God and say look at me…what a good boy am I.

The Lord Jesus had something for them…and it was far from what they expected. In **Matthew chapter 15, beginning in verse 8** he quotes from **Isaiah, chapter 29:13**:

8) "These people draw near to Me **with their mouths**, and **honor Me with their lips**, but their **heart** is far away from Me.
9) And **in vain** they worship Me, teaching as doctrines the commandments of men."

Do you think that God Almighty does not know what lip service is? Of course He does, and He calls it worship that is **"in vain"…a waste of your time and His.**

Worship is not horizontal…look at me, look at you, look at the choir, look at the Pastor. **Worship is vertical**. We come here to **look up** as a body and worship the Father through the Son.

Everything we do here is to say, **"Look at Jesus, look at Jesus, behold the lamb of God, who taketh away the sin of the world."**

Worship is all about the Lord God. He is an **audience of one**.

That's what the Bible calls worship. **We recognize our unworthiness and we recognize the fact that He alone is worthy.**

The fear of the Lord is **recognizing who God is** and how you are incapable of measuring up to that on your own.

3) True worship is about a person and that person is the Father, Son, and Holy Spirit of God.

And when we worship the Lord in truth and spirit, **we must first deal rightly with our sins**.

In the story of the woman at the well, we see that what precedes the discussion about worship is **rightly, the discussion of her immorality**.

She asks Him for a drink of His living water and he tells her to **go get her husband first**. "But I have no husband", is her answer.

If we are going to truly worship God, we have to **deal with sin** and we have to **deal with it rightly**.

There is no such thing as sugar-coated sin. There are no free passes. There is no under-telling the story. Sin is sin. It must be **truthfully accounted for by confessing it to the Father through the Son**… **repented of** (which means to change your ways, do an about face, go the other way) and then and only then receive His forgiveness.

Most of us, like the woman at the well, want to throw a sheet over our short-comings, put some lipstick on that pig, and pretend everything is going to turn out alright.

In Psalm 66:18, King David laments**,** "If I cherish iniquity (wickedness) in my heart, the Lord will not hear me."

If I want to connect with God in worship, **I must first deal rightly with my sin**.

If you try to cover your sin, God will uncover it. Aiken tried that in the Old testament, he stole some items that belonged to God and buried them in his tent.

God then revealed those things to **Joshua** and he was held accountable.

But here's the **good news.** If you come before the Lord in **confession, contrition and true repentance**, God will **cover it in His blood** and remember it no more.

"For I will be merciful to their unrighteousness, and their sins and their lawless deeds. I will remember no more." **Hebrews 8:10**

And He will write his words not upon tablets of stone as in the Old Testament, but on the tablets of your heart. **2 Corinthians 3:3**

He is truly the God who **restores** us all…worthy is He to be **praised**.

Our God is not the God of **unfinished business**. He is the Father who will **bring to completion** the work He began in you.

A new day awaits if you will **open your heart** and **submit your will** to His! Amen.

Source: John MacArthur Radio Broadcast

Credit Where Credit is Not Due

Various Passages

As I look back over a life spent in sales and taking good care of my customers, some of that time was spent **setting up credit accounts** for my larger, commercial customers.

Part of the process is **getting the paperwork filled out, sent to the office**, and then **following through with the company's credit department** to get them approved. After that, I am responsible for **being sure they stay current (and making collections on my own if needed)** all for the purpose of **keeping their credit account in "good standing" with the company.**

Sometimes, getting someone approved for an account took a considerable amount of **lobbying** on my part. I remember one particularly hard-nosed credit manager I worked with who took great pride in calling himself **"the sales prevention department"**.

And of course once they were approved, **more lobbying** was needed **whenever they fell ten days past due.**

I was thinking this week how **our relationship and right-standing with the God who made us** is so much like that…with the glaring exception being, **that none of us are, nor will we ever be, credit-worthy on our own.**

We are considered credit-worthy by grace alone, by Christ alone, and our account, once opened, can never be closed.

Before the beginning of time, God knew us personally and vouched for us. No application was required because there was **nothing** we could put on paper to qualify for an account.

We represented the worst of the worst, someone you'd never bet a nickel on, much less offer a line of credit. Yet unimaginably, our Father in heaven dipped into His vast, uncountable fortune, and **set aside a bankroll for us we've never deserved, to this, or any other day.**

And aren't we blessed to know that **our account representative**, the one who makes intersession for us, the one who stands good for us, is none other than **the Son of God?**.

It is **He** who makes us worthy in the eyes of the Father. It is **He** who opened our account, and **He** who lobbies on our behalf to keep it open for all of eternity.

Worthy of our praise is the Lamb of God, who took our debt upon Himself, **marked it paid-in-full**, and gave us right-standing before the Father.

The entire Word of God, as I heard one preacher say, "From Genesis to Maps" is **dedicated to Jesus, the Messiah**, the son of God who "takes away the debt of the world".

In the Old Testament, Christ is **predicted**. In the New Testament, Christ is **revealed**, In the book of Acts, His church begins and Christ is **preached**. In the epistles, Christ is **explained** by His disciples, and finally, in the book of Revelation, Christ is **expected** to return.

In coming to Christ by faith, God Himself, removes our tattered and threadbare worldly garments and says, **"Here my son or daughter, try this on for size"**, and clothes us in a regal robe of His own making.

His words are soft and tender… "You are now clothed in Christ!"

Galatians 3:27

We recently spent time walking the hills of Rome, as we studied the book of Romans, **easily the greatest account of God's grace** ever written.

Martin Luther called Romans, **"the chief part of the New Testament and truly, the purest gospel"**. In it, the **discovery of God's will for man** and the **depth of His unfathomable love for us,** changed the lives of Luther, John Wesley, John Calvin, William Tyndale and millions of others.

The word of God and the Good News of Jesus the Messiah continues to reach souls into our present day…even in places you would least expect…**like the nation of Israel**.

Recent surveys have revealed thousands of died-in-the-wool Orthodox Jews are now accepting Christ as the Messiah. One recent estimate shows the number at or approaching **one million reformed Jews worldwide.** This is a number that would have been considered **impossible** just a little over seventy years ago. When Israel became a nation again in 1948, the number of Messianic Jews (as they are called) numbered **23**.

Why should this get your attention you ask? If you have your bibles, turn with me to the 7th **chapter of the book of Revelation**:

1) "And after these things I saw four angels standing on the four corners of the earth, holding the four winds of the earth, so that the wind should not blow on the earth, nor on the sea, nor on any tree.

2) And I saw another angel ascending from the east, having the seal of the living God: and he cried with a loud voice to the four angels, to whom it was given to hurt the earth and the sea,

3) saying, "Hurt not the earth, neither the sea, nor the trees, till we have sealed the servants of our God in their foreheads.

4) And I heard the number of them that were sealed: and there were **a hundred and forty and four thousand** of all the tribes of the children of Israel.

So in the last days, as Tribulation judgment falls on planet earth, **God seals 144,000** of the nation of Israel (12,000 from each of the 12 tribes) for the sole purpose of **evangelizing the world**.

Now I ask you…how could He seal 144,000 Christ-accepting, Christ-believing Jews for this purpose if they did not exist?

Therefore the news of today…one million Messianic Jews and counting tells us "Christ is on the way, even at the door".

Halleluiah!, come quickly Lord Jesus!

In everything, God does **what we cannot do**, so we **can be what we dare to dream**: perfect and in right-standing with Him. All this, while making it known that it is **His will that every man** should come to this knowledge and be saved.

In assuming a **debt** we stand accountable for, Jesus doesn't just **sweep** it under the carpet, He puts it **under His blood**.

Because of this, God **imputes** His righteousness to our account and we become children of God and heirs to His riches in glory.

Simply put, **we are given credit where credit is not due.**

God's credit requirements are **met** by Christ's sacrifice. His holiness is **honored**. Our **debt is paid**, never to be remembered again, and we are **redeemed** and allowed direct access to His throne.

If you've ever wondered how long God's love for you might last, you'll find your answer on a **splinter-filled cross at Calvary** so long ago.

That's **Him** up there, your maker, your God, nailed and bleeding, spit on and accursed. That's **your** death He's dying. That's **your** bill **He's** paying. That's **your** life he's resurrecting.

That's how much He loves you.

All of this leads to a **better understanding** of what our future hope is in Christ, thanks to the **loving grace and mercy that God bestowed on us**. For even as we walk this earth and face the many challenges here below, **our spiritual position is in the heavenly realms where we are seated with our Lord and Savior, Jesus Christ.**

And God did all of this before the beginning of time so that in the coming ages, **His exceedingly incomprehensible and incomparable riches and kindness** toward us will be on display for all to see...**for all eternity!**

To Him be the honor, and the glory, forever and ever. Amen

Directions: Don't Leave Home Without Them

Various Passages

With the advent of today's Global Positioning System, or GPS, and it's availability on cell phones, Ipads, and even automobile dashboards, "getting lost" has pretty much become a thing of the past.

I know someone who refuses to go to the mailbox without it. She finds the audible voice soothing, comforting, trustworthy, and dependable.

For most of my life, I preferred to get a general idea of the targeted location, and then use the **"figure it out as we go"** method…no more. I have become a GPS convert in it's purest form.

There are people who say the nation of Israel wandered the wilderness for forty years because the men **would not stop and ask for directions**.

It is then safe to say, that if you want to get where you are going… **getting directions**…and most importantly…**getting the proper directions**…is the only way to go.

In the world in which we live, there are millions of people who think they know where they are going when they die. Unfortunately, **they don't have a clue** what they're talking about.

Why?…because they **have not stopped long enough** (nor invested the time) to get the **proper directions**.

Even though there is available information at their fingertips, from multiple sources, they are flying blind in the **"figure it out as we go"** lane.

It is this lane, this going-fast-to-nowhere lane, that our Savior describes in **Matthew 7:13: "For wide is the gate, and broad is the way that leads to destruction, and many there are who go that way."**

We all know people on this road.

The next chance you get, ask them this: "Do you know that the God who made you, loves you, **and** has a plan for your life?"

Then play close attention to their answer.

Because most people want to act like they know where they're going. They want to look the part, even though they may be lost in the forest of this world. They are blinded, deceived, over-flowing with bad information, and rolling on that superhighway of destruction. But they have all their friends, they have all their stuff, and have swallowed the bait (which is hiding the hook) that says they are A-ok!…instead of being here with us hearing the Word.

Speaking of which, let's open our bibles and see what the Word of God has to say. Let's see what our creator would have us know today about getting directions.

Today, we'll go old school. Chuck Swindoll refuses to call it the Old Testament. He says that makes it sound dated and of no use to us today. He calls it the Older Testament and follows that with the Newer Testament. I like the way he thinks.

Psalm 23 NIV
1) "The Lord is my shepherd, I lack nothing.
2) He makes me lie down in green pastures, he leads me beside still waters,
3) he refreshes my soul. He guides me along the right paths for His names sake.

Here we see God's plan for all of us is to refresh our souls and guide us along the right path back to Him.

That is why Christ came to begin with…to restore all of humanity back to the path God originally designed for us…the path of righteousness.

But before anyone can accomplish this and receive this free gift, there has to be some time spent reading the directions.

Psalm 32:8 and 10 NIV
8) "I will instruct you and teach you in the way you should go; I will counsel you with loving eye upon you.
10) Many are the sorrows of the wicked, but the LORD's unfailing love surrounds the one who trusts in Him."

The Father, Himself, will teach us His ways, His wisdom. His eyes will forever be upon us. His love surrounds us. These are the promises of His word.

This does not apply to those who care nothing for His words or wisdom. They can look forward to many sorrows…in this life and especially in the spirit-life to come.

Psalm 119: NIV
1) Blessed are those whose ways are blameless, who walk according to the law of the Lord.
2) Blessed are those who keep His statutes and seek Him with all their heart-
3) they do no wrong to follow His ways.

104) I gain understanding from your precepts; therefore I hate every wrong path.
105) Your word is a lamp unto my feet, a light on my path.

If you are wandering around in the dark, even in your own yard, you do well to **get yourself a flashlight** so you can see where you are going.

For the Christian, the follower of Christ, **the word of God is a lamp unto our feet and a light on our path.** Here in the bible, by the power of the Holy Spirit, writers have been inspired to record the most intimate thoughts of Jehovah God. **His thoughts. His directions.**

All for the purpose of guiding us through this **field full of land mines** we call modern life.

Proverbs 4:10 and following: (paraphrased)
10) "Hear, oh my son, and **receive my sayings**; and the years of your life shall be many.
11) I have taught you **in the way of wisdom**; I have led you **in right paths**.
12) Wherever you go, your steps **will not be hindered**, and when you run you **will not stumble**.
13) Take fast hold of **My instruction**; do not let go: keep it for this is **your life**.
20) My son, attend my words; incline your ear **to my sayings**,
21) do not let them **leave your eyes**: keep them **in the midst of your heart**.
22) For they are **life** to those that find them and in them **is good health**."

How many times a day do you hear the call of the world trying to pull you this way or that? "Hey, come over here, do this, or do that, and you will be very happy!...don't be so uptight following all of those man-made rules in the bible...come, be with all your friends and enjoy this life...yanno, you only go around once...let's make the most of it!"

This is the great deception that the herd follows. Again, the wide superhighway of destruction.

Romans 10:17
"Faith comes by hearing and hearing by the word of God."

Proverbs tells us to walk in His council and things **will be well with you**.

So tell me, how can we ever know if this is true if we never find time to **read or hear His words**?

Now here's the **bad news**. Everyone of us has **issues**. I see no need to go through the litany of descriptions of what these can be. You know it, and I know it…**we all have issues**.

My point here is, unless you are constantly putting yourself under the blood of Christ and hiding His words in your heart, you are sentencing yourself to a lifetime of **succumbing** to these temptations, whatever they may be…which means living a life in bondage to the flesh.

That is why from the best of us to the worst of us, we need **God's GPS directing us through each and every day**.

How many times have you been knee-deep in some type of trial or temptation…may it through to daylight…and said, "Ok, God…thanks, I got it from here"…**only to fall flat on your face** two days later?

And what are our directions?…what does God's GPS say?

Isaiah 30:21
"And your ears shall hear a word behind you, saying, this is the way, walk in it."

How are you going to hear this word, these directions, if you're walking around with your GPS turned off?

Jeremiah 6:16

"Thus says the LORD, "**Stand in the way**, and ask for the old paths, **where is the good way**, and **walk therein**, and you will find rest for your souls." But the people said, "No, we will not walk therein."

Stop blaming God for your troubles. **Stop** blaming God for your unhappiness. He has provided you with a perfectly good GPS system and you **won't even turn it on!**

Amos 8:11 and 12

11) "Behold, the days are coming, says the LORD God, that I will send a famine in the land, not a famine of bread, nor a thirst for water, **but of hearing the words of the Lord;**

12) and they will wander from sea to sea, and from north to south, they will run to and fro to seek the word of the LORD, **and they will not find it.**"

You only have to hear one commentary of today describe the word of God as **"hate speech"** to know the day just detailed by the prophet Amos is rapidly approaching.

Read your bible. Talk to your God. Stay in the word. Get some good directions or you are going to end up in the swamp with everybody else…and I'm not talking about Ben Hill Stadium.

The time to choose is now. Take the next exit, **get some new directions**, and find the way that **leads to the narrow gate**.

Amen.

Source: Insight For Living, Charles Swindoll
        Radio Broadcast

"The True Vine"

John, Chapter 15

Last week we talked about the importance of **getting directions** …and not just any directions, **the proper directions**.

An example of this would be:

What good would it do for you to leave home hoping to end up in Atlanta, while using the directions that would take you to Miami?

And we talked about the modern day GPS system and the **value it** represents to present day travel.

But we also asked the question, "What good would it do to have access to this system and **never put it to use**?"

The longer I study God's word, and hear His messages preached daily on the radio and television, the more I am impressed by the fact that following Jesus, truly giving one's self over to living your life through Him, involves establishing an **ever-strengthening bond** or **relationship** with Him.

Knowing Him thoroughly and intimately, can only be achieved by allowing yourself to be **awash** in Him. **Studying** Him. **Praying** to Him. **Listening** for Him. **Relishing** Him.

The shortest route to this kind of relationship with the one who laid down His life for us so long ago…so that we may be redeemed spotless in the eyes of His Father…is to **constantly** work our way through His recorded words in the four gospels.

Jesus himself said, "Every word that comes out of a man's mouth is what makes him…not what he puts in his stomach." **(paraphrased)**

If you have your bibles, let's turn together to the **15ᵗʰ Chapter of John, beginning in verse 1**.

Here we find Jesus speaking, and presenting the last of seven **"I am"** statements recorded by John in his gospel account.

1) "I am the **true vine** and my Father is the **vine-dresser**.
2) Every branch in Me that does not bear fruit He takes away; and every branch that bears fruit He prunes, that it may bear more fruit.
4) Abide in Me, and I in you. As the branch cannot bear fruit of itself, unless it **abides** in the vine, neither can you, unless you **abide** in Me.
5) I am the vine, **you are the branches**. He who **abides** in Me, and I in him, bears much fruit; for without Me **you can do nothing**."

As I've told you before, my mother was a gardener and had a yard full of fruit-bearing trees.

She also had fifty feet of grape vines in the front yard (times 2) and an aging grape arbor of about the same length in the back. Every year, I was not a happy camper around late February/March, because it was time to prune the vines ahead of the spring and summer growing season. It was an arduous task to begin with, and then once done, the cuttings had to be rounded up, piled up, and burned.

In this **15ᵗʰ Chapter of John**, Jesus is teaching his disciples about relationships.

In the first **eleven verses**, He is talking about our relationship with Him. In the next **six verses** He is talking about our relationship with other Christians. Then, in the last **ten verses** He is talking about our relationship with the world.

Working our way up from the bottom, the Lord uses the word **"hate"** eight times…as in…they **hate me**, therefore, they will **hate you**. When the Lord uses a word this many times, it is worth our attention.

He is emphasizing that there will be a "hate" relationship between the **people of God** and the **people of the world**. Will you stand with him when this kind of emotion comes your way?

We recently watched a program on TBN that detailed some of the persecution of believers in our world today…especially in the Communist countries. Rest assured this type of oppression is **working its way** into the very fabric of the United States through an assorted agenda of **liberal ideology**. It is no longer conjecture, but fact, that what will follow is **religious oppression** and **persecution** of the Christian faith. This is the playbook they are following…so the time to prepare our hearts and minds is **now**.

In the middle section, **verses twelve through seventeen**, the key word is **"love"**. "You will **love me**, you will **love each other**, you will **love other brothers and sisters of the faith**."

In **verses one through eleven**, the key word is **"abide"**. Ten times in eleven verses he uses this word.

If you want to relate correctly with Christ, our Risen Savior, then you want to know what it means to **"abide"**.

These first eleven verses are for **believers** only. These will be our focus today.

When I say for "believers only", it doesn't mean the world can't hear the words...**it simply means the world has no ability to "abide" in Him**. This is not the place for a non-believer to turn and find out how to be a Christian..."abiding" will seem as foolishness to them.

For us, the ones already "in Christ", this chapter is the place to turn to find out **how to walk with God**.

These verses are symbolic. We are told about the relationship between **the vine and the branch**. We are told how the vinedresser **prunes and works with the branches on the vine** to produce the best crop of fruit...and we, are these branches.

This example of a vine and it's branches is replete in the Older Testament. **Isaiah, Jeremiah, Hosea, and Ezekiel** all refer to the nation of Israel as a vine...and in each instance, the LORD is concerned about it. He wants it to flourish, grow, and prosper under His guidance.

Yet, because of the **unfaithfulness and rebellion** of the nation, the vine **withered** and **floundered**. This allowed the **Gentiles**, you and me, to be grafted into the vine...and now that we have been graciously grafted in, The Lord God above **expects us to grow, flourish and produce** good fruit. Do not be lulled into believing that the Lord God is not also watching and evaluating the branches known as the United States of America, who He has blessed abundantly over the last two hundred plus years. He continues to keep His **pruning shears** at hand...and He knows how to use them.

Now, let's come full circle and get back to this term **"abide"** the Lord uses so liberally in these passages.

These eleven verses are not about the **root**, but the **fruit**. He is not talking about a path to salvation here, that is already assumed in His audience...He is talking about productivity...the **fruit** that is produced by the **branches**, through the life of the vine.

Here Jesus is telling His disciples, and through them to us, that the entire purpose of this relationship between the vine and it's branches is to **produce more fruit**.

As a result of abiding in Christ there will be the bearing of fruit… and you don't have to sit and wonder about the identity of the vine…he tells us in the first two words…**"I am"**.

6) "If anyone **does not abide** in Me he is **cast out** as a branch and is withered; and they gather them and throw them into the fire, and they are burned.
7) If you **abide** in me and My words **abide** in you, you will ask what you desire and it **shall be done for you**.
8) By this My Father is glorified, **that you bear much fruit**; so you will be My disciples."

True believers **obey the Lord's commands** and **submit their will to His Word**. Because of their **commitment** to God's Word, they are **devoted** to His will, **their prayers are fruitful**, and God's **full glory** is put on display.

It is **impossible** according to this passage to be a branch and not be "in Christ". It is possible, however, to be a branch that is **not producing fruit**. When we came to know Jesus as Lord, the Father grafted us into the vine (Him). This means we are **drawing our life** from the Lord Jesus that we might be acceptable before God.

But this is only part of the story.

Verse two talks about being **"in"** Him. **Verse four** talks about **"abiding"** in Him and producing fruit. We are never **commanded** to be **"in the vine"**, but we are **commanded to "abide"** once there…all for the purpose of being productive.

Being **"in Christ"** simply marks our **position**. **"Abiding"** in Christ is what **is expected** to the glory of the Father…**which is reproducing the character of Christ in us**.

The life of Christ flows through the vine and into us, the branches. **Therefore, what characterized His life should begin to characterize ours…to love God with all your heart and soul and to love one another as yourself.**

The words of the bible have a **detergent element** to them. The more you pour through the scriptures, the more **cleansing effect** they have on the reader. It begins to seem as if our creator is speaking directly to us…as if He wrote this passage just for us.

Let's move to **Hebrews, chapter 4, verse 12**:
12) "For the word of God **is living and powerful**, and **sharper than any two-edged sword**, piercing even to the division of soul and spirit, and of joints and marrow, and is a discerner of the thoughts and intents of the heart.

We must never forget that while the Word of God is **comforting** and **nourishing** to those who believe, it is also a **tool of judgment** to those who do not believe. It also **exposes shallow beliefs** and **false intentions** by examining the heart which can hide nothing from His eyes.

God's word has the ability to guide us to the very falsehood and sin problem we may be experiencing and then get rid of it.

This is more than good directions. More than GPS. This is our **Creator**, through **His son Jesus**, and by the **power of the Holy Spirit**, fast-tracking us for **a better life, a more fruitful life** and **preparing us for a personal relationship** that will last for all of eternity and beyond. Amen.

Part II

Last week as we studied **John, Chapter 15** we learned that a result of **abiding in Christ** is the **bearing of fruit**.

We learned that Jesus is the vine and His father is the vine dresser. So the Father is the one who works with the branches **(you and me)** that we may produce **even more fruit**.

Viticulture is the cultivation of grape vines for the purpose of harvesting grapes for eating or to be made into wine. Besides planting new vines, fertilizing and watering, viticulture consists mainly of pruning.

And in pruning, two principles are generally observed:
1) Dead wood must be removed ruthlessly.
2) Live wood must be cut back drastically.

Dead wood contains insects and disease that could threaten to destroy the entire vine if left unheeded.

Live wood must be cut back to the extent that the nourishment of the vine goes into the grapes and not simply making more, bigger wood.

As the wine grower cuts back his arbors, so does God prune His branches to the extent that it may seem cruel to the casual observer.

Nevertheless, from those who often suffer the most comes the most special fruit. Don't believe me?...google Joni Erickson Tada this week... learn about her life and ministry.

Have you ever felt that the Father has cut you back so far that the stumps He left were bleeding? I have...and it wasn't fun.

But I must admit, that much later, out of that, came a wonderful crop of sweet, full, fruit.

We don't like the pruning. We resist the knife. We see countless others that (we feel) need it more that us. But the Father is the dresser...only He knows the beginning from the end. Only He can see the crop that will come from His work with us.

"He that abides in Me and Me in him produces much fruit. Apart from me you can do nothing."

But we don't believe that. We are too gifted. So we work even harder on our own to produce fruit!...grunting from the effort along the way.

Let me ask you. Have you ever heard a fruit tree grunt? I can take you to the orange orchards of Central Florida and you won't hear a sound. There they are, mile after mile, row after row, silently producing glorious oranges. All this, after the dresser has does his work.

We can do many things without depending on Christ. Our flesh can produce much fruit by the sack full. This doesn't mean, however, that it will be right for the table...or even consumable for that matter. It will be a phony imitation of the real thing and anyone with a thimble of discernment will call you out and turn from your company.

These fleshly works will be rounded up as verse six says, "cast away and thrown into the fire."

Let's scoot over to **1 Corinthians 3:13 and beyond**, The Living Bible
13) "There is going to come a day of testing at Christ's Judgment Day to see what kind of material every builder used. Everyone's work will be put through the fire so that all can see whether or not it keeps its value, and what was really accomplished.
14) Then, every workman who has built on the foundation with the right materials, and whose work stands, will get his pay.
15) But if the house he has built burns up, he will suffer great loss. He himself will be saved, but like a man escaping through a wall of smoke."

This is a companion verse to **John, chapter 15** and helps expound on the subject of abiding in Christ.

When we abide in Christ, we "trust in"…we "lean on" Christ. We rely upon Him to draw our motivation and direction for life.

We should start every day in prayer like this: "Lord Jesus, thank you for this day you've given me…and now I give it back to you. The hours that are in front of me are yours. I want this day to be drawn from the deepest well that is you and I want to accomplish what you have set forth for me to do."

Proverbs 3:5-6
5) "Trust in the LORD with all your heart and lean not unto your own understanding.
6) In all your ways acknowledge Him, and He will make smooth and straight your path."

As long as your house is connected to the power source or station, you will live with the lights on…but lose that connection…even for a few seconds and you are in the darkest dark.

The same principle applies concerning your relationship with the Lord. Stay connected. Stay in prayer. Stay in the word.

The bible tells us to resist the devil and he is required to flee.
The apostle Paul tells us to take off the old man and put on the new, and that if we be found in Christ, we become a new creation.
Walking worthy of this appointment is your reasonable sacrifice.
Walk in it.

Refusing to abide produces barrenness, disassociation, desolation.
Don't chance it.

Even Moses said, "Sin has its pleasure for a season." The key phrase there is "pleasure for a season"…and then what?

I personally know the answer to that question: barrenness, disassociation, desolation.

Again, don't chance it.

The scars are deep and the road back is long and hard. The Lord promises to restore the years the locust have eaten but it isn't overnight… and some losses are never regained.

The time of pleasure does not begin to offset the pain of the whirlwind. What is sowed, must be reaped and the scars are there forever.

When Christ asked the twelve, "Will you also go away?", Peter answered, "Lord, to whom shall we go?…you have the words of eternal life." Be like Peter.

Refusing to abide is barrenness…don't chance it.
The result of abiding is fruitfulness…don't miss it.

Verse 11) "These things I have spoken to you that MY joy might remain in you and your joy might be full."
Amen.

Father thank you for pruning us when we need it…and even when we feel we don't.
Thank you for lifting us up from the soil, cleaning us up, and repositioning us on the vine.
Thank you for your forgiveness that comes upon confession.
Thank you for remembering our sins no more.

Thank you for the hope of eternal life that comes as a gift from your Holy Spirit.

And father, may the days to come be filled with joy and abundant living. Create in us a pure heart, Father, and hide your precious word there.

May our motives be pure, may our days be prosperous in your service.

May we leave here today with a refreshed, renewed walk with you. May our thoughts be cleaner. May our actions stem from a desire to glorify you…regardless of the outcome.

We pray in Jesus name. Amen

Sources: Insight for Living,
              Charles Swindoll Radio Broadcast
              John MacArthur Study Bible

"An Intimate Conversation With Jesus"
A One Act Play December 23, 2023

Shalom, My brothers and sisters of the faith at Sharon Baptist Church! Glory to God in the highest, and on earth, goodwill among men with whom He is well pleased!

Again I say Shalom!
This is to say, My peace I give to you…not as the world gives…but as only I can give. This is also a prayer…and a blessing I bring for you tonight. I wish you wholeness and well-being as you gather to celebrate Me…and My Father who sent me.

I have come to you tonight to speak on many topics.
I have heard the world saying I can only be one of three…a LIAR, a LUNATIC…or THE LORD…the Son of the Living God.
I can assure you that I am indeed the latter.
And there are great rewards for those that confess this with their mouths and believe this with their hearts.

I am the good shepherd and as all good shepherds, I know my sheep and they know Me…I call them by name and they come to Me…just as My Father knows Me and I know Him.

He has given me the authority to lay down my life for my sheep…for you…and pick it up again, which I have done so many years ago.

Because of this sacrifice, freely given, I am the resurrection and the life. Whosoever believes this, though he may die, yet will he live again.

This is My promise offered to you…and from My Father in heaven who sent Me. Hold fast to this promise.

Let not your heart be troubled, neither be afraid…for My word is good…and I am with you even to the end of the world.

I am the bread of life. No one who comes to Me will ever hunger again…and whosoever believes in me will never thirst again. Receive the Holy Spirit and rivers of living water will flow from you as you bless others.

Through Me you may enter the very throne of Grace boldly and stand before your Father in heaven, asking anything believing and it will be given unto you…for it pleases the Father to give good gifts to His children.

Do you not know by now that I am the way, the truth, and the life? And that no one comes to the Father but through Me?

This is no small statement…for it was and is a stumbling block to the Jews…and it was and is foolishness to the Gentile.

Yet to you, my disciples, it has been revealed by the power of God's Holy Spirit as truth.

Do not be led astray by those who say you must check your brain at the door to come in and worship God.

I tell you truly, they will be the fools on Judgment Day, for it pleases the Father to confound the haughty and the prideful with the simple message of redemption.

I am the narrow door, the single passage way from this life to life everlasting.

He that believes this and hides it in his heart will live abundantly in this life…and through Me will receive bountiful everlasting rewards in the life to come.

I am the sole mediator between God and all of humanity.

I am also the advocate who represents you in heaven, just as the Holy Spirit does so here on earth.

Always remember, I am coming quickly and My rewards are with Me. Know this: because of Me, you have been made more than conquerors and will rule alongside Me when I come into My kingdom.

I am the light of the world. Whosoever follows me will not walk in darkness but will have the light of life.

Do you not understand that you have been made joint heirs with Me… subject to inherit the vast riches of My Father?

Do you not know that you will one day be placed in a position to judge the actions of the angels in heaven?

I urge you to live a life worthy of the calling you have received. Be completely humble and gentle; be patient, bearing one another in love. You are considered as royalty before the Father because of His love and grace for you…now go and walk worthy of your position.

I am the true vine and My Father is the vine dresser.

At His will, He discards branches that are not producing fruit, and prunes those that are…that they may produce even more.

The fields are full but the harvesters are few.

Pray the Father will send you into the fields to harvest.

If you abide in Me, I will abide in you, all for the purpose of showing you things which you do not know…that you may come to the knowledge of God.

I will teach you the ways of wisdom, and cause you to take the right paths. I will make smooth and straight the road ahead of you.

So continue to fight the good fight and run a good race…stay the course…and rewards will be stored for you in My Father's house that will never know tarnish nor rust.

In My Father's house there are many rooms and I have gone there to prepare a place just for you...so that where I am, there you may be also. Life everlasting with Me lies just ahead for those who are mine.
I am the Master, and when the Master returns He will be looking for you...standing at the edge of the clearing with your lamps lit awaiting My arrival.

Do not be distracted or led astray. Shut out false teachers who would come and steal your inheritance.
Be aware that in the last days, scoffers will come who are living by their own wicked ways and say, "So Jesus promised to come back did he?... then where is HE?"

For as far back as anyone can remember everything has remained exactly the same since the first day of creation!"

They are deceivers and were it possible they would even deceive you... my elect!

I am the good shepherd who protects the flock...but there are wolves about.
The God they desire is not the God they require.
They secretly desire to be God themselves...they have no need of the one true God and His offer of redemption and salvation.

Know them by their actions, their words, their deeds and do not give them ear. Instead, I encourage you to stay with the flock, the body of Christ.

Together, celebrate My truths, encourage and watch over one another, yeah, love one another. By this all men will know that you are mine... that you love one another.

The world will tell you to hate your enemies...even the non-believers can do this. I will tell you to love your enemies and pray for them. The Father in heaven will hear you and be pleased by this action.

I am the fulfillment of all prophesy. I am the completion of God's work with man. I have come to seek and save the lost. I am the One to Come, the Messiah, The Lion of Judah, The Prince of Peace, the King of all Kings, the Lord of all Lords.

When the fullness of time had come,..
I am the Word become flesh…and I dwelt among you.

But I am also the Lamb of God, the living sacrifice, who shed His blood for the remission of your sins, thereby "paying in full" a debt you could never repay.

This was the redemptive plan of My Father since the beginning of time…that I may be the first fruits of the many that follow Me.
Though none were worthy, no not one, He has taken your sins that were scarlet and washed them white as fine wool, remembering them no more.
Like the Father of the returning prodigal son, He has seen you coming from afar off and run to meet you. He has dressed you in royal robes and placed His ring upon your finger.

Because of this, there is now no condemnation for those of you in me.

There is no power in the sky above, nor the earth below…there is nothing in all of creation that will be able to separate you from the love of God.

Again, I say unto you, I am the good shepherd and those the Father has given Me, I will never let them go.

When you are gathered together, I will be among you. When you lay you head on your pillow, I will give you rest. When you come to Me in prayer, I will be listening.

Your faith will be ever-strengthened by my words and will allow you to stand during times of testing. Hide them in your hearts, put on the full armor of God, and stand firm against the enemy.

Soon, I will return and gather you unto myself. What a glorious, joyous time that will be! You cannot possibly imagine all that My Father has set aside for that moment…just for you…out of His vast riches.

The entire heavenly host, ten thousand times ten thousand and thousands and thousands more excitedly await your arrival.

Your friends, your neighbors, your loved ones that believed in Me and have preceded you in death are also waiting to receive you.

Though they are absent from the body, they are present with me now…
as we speak.
What a wondrous reunion that will be!
So I say again,…stay the course…finish the race.

YOU are the children of God, the redeemed, the resurrected, the refreshed, the renewed, the restored. You are the ones all of heaven has waited for…eons upon eons…time immortal.

YOU are the beginning of a celebration that will know no end. For YOU are the ones chosen,…known, loved, and cherished by My Father before you were ever born.

YOU are the reason for this season!…For GOD so loved the world!

This is the great hope of the gospel message. This is My story, My life.

Believe in Me and I will live again through you. Together, there is nothing we cannot do.

I long to welcome you, My brothers and sisters, to My great reward.

May the God of hope fill you with all joy and peace as you trust in Him, so that you may overflow with hope by the power of the Holy Spirit.

Before I take my leave, I would like to pray a blessing over you all.

Our Father, in heaven, blessed be Your name. May your kingdom soon come to earth, may your will be done, as it already exists in heaven.

Give each of these here tonight bountiful provisions for the day to come. Comfort them that are weary or troubled, Father….Heal those that are sick. Bless those that are faithful and continue to reveal yourself to them through the work of your Holy Spirit.

Forgive them their trespasses, Father and help them to be loving and forgiving to those who trespass against them. Teach them to be peace makers, Father…and give them humble, gentle, joyful spirits.

Do not allow them to be led into temptation. Deliver them swiftly from the schemes of the evil one.

Together, Father,…tonight, we honor you Father for your long-suffering,…your loving kindness…and for revealing yourself to us. May your kingdom come soon… in all power and in all glory…sweeping away the old…making all things new…
and may it know no end!

Amen

Until we meet again my brothers and sisters on that great day of reunion---

Shalom!…my peace I leave with you!

Getting a Good Start, Welcoming the New Year

Joshua 1: 1-9

Anyone who has ever run track, or cross country, or even marathons, will tell you that the most important part of the race is **getting a good start**.

It doesn't matter at that moment how much training you've had, how much you may have studied the course, or how many times before you may have run that particular race.

What matters most, in that one moment in time when the gun goes off, **is getting a good start**.

I would share with you this morning that I had a sermon prepared in advance for today, in fact enough for the next two Sundays, as it was my intention to begin leading us through a verse-by-verse study of the Gospel of John…which we will indeed begin soon in the new year.

But all this week, I have felt the Lord nudging me in another direction for today…and that is how we should **prepare our hearts and minds** for the start of a new race, **one called 2023**.

And in just the same way as preparing for a track and field event, our focus today for 2023 is going to be **getting off to a good start**…
specifically in our relationship with our Lord and Savior, Jesus Christ…and through Him by the prompting of the Holy Spirit…

improving our relationship with our forgiving, long-suffering Father, Jehovah God.

If you have your bibles, turn with me to **Joshua, chapter 1**.

1) "Now after the death of Moses the servant of the LORD, it came to pass, that the LORD spoke unto Joshua the son of Nun, Moses' minister, saying,

2) Moses my servant is dead; now therefore arise, go over this Jordan, you and all this people, unto the land which I do give them, even to the children of Israel.

3) Every place that the sole of your foot shall walk upon; that I have given you, as I said to Moses.

4) From the wilderness and this Lebanon even unto the great river Euphrates, all the land of the Hittites, and unto the great sea toward the going down of the sun, shall be your coast.

5) There shall not any man be able to stand before you all the days of your life: as I was with Moses, so I will be with you: I will not fail you, nor foresake you.

6) Be strong and of good courage: for unto this people shall you divide for an inheritance the land, which I swore unto their fathers to give them.

7) Only be strong and courageous, that you may observe to do according to all the law, which Moses my servant commanded you: turn not from it to the right hand or the left, that you may prosper wherever you go.

8) This book of the law should not depart from your mouth; but you should meditate therein day and night: for then you will make your way prosperous, and then will you have good success.

9) Have I not commanded you? Be strong and of good courage; be not afraid, neither be dismayed: for the LORD your God is with you wherever you go."

Before we look at the passage, let's review what has happened:

The LORD (and anytime you see it written this was in the Old Testament it is referencing the LORD God Jehovah) is speaking to Joshua. **Why?**…because in **verse 1 and 2** we find out that his leader, **Moses, is dead**.

Now this is no small thing. We are talking about **Moses**. The same one who went before Pharaoh, the same one who performed miracles in Pharaoh's court, the same one who led approximately two million people out of Egypt who had been held captive for 400 years, the same one who God personally gave stone tablets containing the ten commandments…and so on and so on. **Moses!…**the leader of the nation Israel for over 40 years is dead!

And now you, Joshua, are the **"next man up"**.

If you follow the game of football at all you are familiar with the term **"next man up"**. Football is and has always been a violent sport producing unending injuries on a large scale.

For a team to succeed in any league they have to be able to overcome these injuries when valuable players are sidelined. What makes this possible is the **"next man up"** program where backup players are ready to move in and contribute when called upon to do so.

So right away in **Joshua, Chapter 1**, the sixth book in the bible, we see that Joshua has been hand selected by God to be the **"next man up"** and lead the nation Israel after the death of their revered leader, Moses.

The value in this passage for us today, is that the same promises God made to Joshua, are **still alive and well for us today**.

As Joshua faced the daunting task of crossing a river and leading a nation into uncharted territory, we as the body of Christ are facing a crossing of our own…from the known year 2022…into the unknown year of 2023.

Without the ability to raise Moses from the dead, Joshua had to bring himself to a point where he could release what was behind him and trust God to bring him into a new reality with new possibilities. We have the same opportunity before us today as we step forward into the New Year.

No one drives a motor vehicle while continuously looking in the **rear view mirror**. To do so is a wreck looking for a place to happen. You drive looking out of the **front windshield** as your vehicle is moving you ahead from point A to point B. You may check the rear view mirror occasionally as a reference to where you've been, but the lions' share of your attention should be spent looking where you are going.

In the **spiritual world**, this is called **trusting God**…and **laying claim to His promises**. Maybe your 22' was filled with happiness, or maybe sadness, or a mixture of both…regardless, you cannot allow for a fresh start to 23' if you are dragging a bag of happenstance with you from 22' that you cannot change.

All that will accomplish is ruining the most important part of the race ahead…**the good start**.

In **Joshua Chapter 1**, I want to first draw your attention to the ending promises of verses 7, 8, and 9.
Verse 7) "that you may prosper wherever you go"
Verse 8) "for then you will make your way prosperous and then you will have good success"
Verse 9) "be not afraid, neither be dismayed: For the LORD your God is with you wherever you go"

Now let's imagine we aren't reading promises that were given to one of God's servants over three thousand years ago. Let's pretend God has called you off the bench and given these promises to you today.

Obviously the next question one might ask is… "Ok, what is required of me so that I might receive these promises?"

As it was over three thousand years ago… it is today.

"I am the LORD", he says, "I change not". **Malachi 3:6**

In this passage from long ago, we see God telling Joshua that **now is the time** to cross the Jordan and lead the nation into the land that was promised to them…

that every step he takes will be on land **he should claim** and that **no man** will be able to stand against him in this effort. "You saw how I was with Moses", He proclaims, "and so will I be with you".

Three times in the last four verses He tells Joshua to be **"strong and courageous"…**all the while hiding the Law **(His word)** in his heart. This should be accomplished by Joshua "meditating on it day and night", He says.

Therefore, we see that God tells Joshua that he will be successful as long as:
1) God is glorified in all that He accomplishes
2) That God's people are benefitted
3) and that God's kingdom is expanded.

Over three thousand years later, are these not our marching orders for today? No matter how much success you amass in the world today, if God is not glorified by it, if people (other than yourself) are not benefitted, and it does nothing to expand God's kingdom, what have you really accomplished?

So here are four keys to success as God defined it to Joshua and through him, as He defines it to us today.

1) Leave yesterday behind.
"Moses my servant is dead, therefore arise and cross the Jordan". **Moses is gone and he's not coming back…get up, and get moving.**

Today marks day one of a brand new year. A year that the Lord has already planned for you. A year the Lord already knows the beginning, the end and everything in between. **Leave last year at the door,** don't drag it into this year as unnecessary weight. It is done and over with.

Don't be held hostage by yesterday. Be ready when the Lord calls for the **"next man up"** and get a **good start** as you go into 2023.

2) Seize your inheritance.

Lay claim to you allotted portion. Every believer has been given an **allotted portion of time, talent, and treasures** for the purpose of fulfilling God's will for your life, and expanding His kingdom.

When Joshua was to lead the people over the Jordan river, there was a section of property for each of the twelve tribes of Israel.

This was their inheritance. This was their allotted land. But notice this: **it was land that was already inhabited so they had to trust God and go get it**.

God told him "everywhere you put your foot will be your land"

Or,…another way…"I have it to give to you, but you have to **get up and go get it."**

God's promises are often in your reach, but not in your hand.

In 2023 **get up and go** get your inheritance that God already has prepared for you.

3) Focus on God, not man.

Why does God say three times for Joshua to be "strong and courageous?

Because when He told Joshua to cross the Jordan to take the land he had waiting on them, and when you today, cross over into a brand new unknown year, **God knows you will encounter spiritual resistance**. Satan and his followers do not want you to lay hands on your inheritance. He does not want you to accomplish one thing to further God's kingdom.

That is why he will throw every stumbling block he can your way so you will take your eyes off God and be mesmerized by troubling circumstances. If he can do that, he has you on your way to defeat.

The **only person** who can stop what God has for you, **is you**.

God told Joshua and through him he tells us, "**no man** will be able to stand before you all the days of your life".

This is why a relationship with the Lord is so important. This is **assignment** coupled with **His Presence**...**verse 9**... "for the Lord your God is with you wherever you go."

Don't go after the **promise** without **His Presence** in 2023.

4) You must stay tethered to God's word.
Verse 7 "observe to do according to the law, which Moses My servant commanded you: do not turn from it to the right or to the left"
Verse 8 "do not let it depart from your mouth and meditate on it day and night"

Here, God says of His word:
1) Proclaim it (let it not depart from your mouth)
2) Possess it (meditate on it day and night)
3) Practice it (let it lead your way so you do not wander off to the right or to the left)

Start today. Begin 2023 with a promise to yourself to:
Leave yesterday behind.
Seize your inheritance.
Focus on your relationship with God
Stay tethered to His word.

And see what a difference it will make.
Amen

Source: Tony Evans Radio Broadcast

Sermon, June 4, 2023
Anxious About Nothing

Philippians 4: 4-13 (Living Bible)

4) "Always be full of joy in the Lord. I say it again, rejoice!

5) Let everyone see that you are unselfish and considerate in all you do. Remember that the Lord is coming soon.

6) Don't worry about anything; instead pray about everything; tell God your needs and don't forget to thank Him for His answers.

7) If you do this you will experience God's peace, which is far more wonderful than the human mind can understand. His peace will keep your hearts and mind quiet and at rest as you trust in Christ Jesus

8) And now brothers, as I close this letter let me say this one more thing: Fix your thoughts on what is true and good and right. Think about things that are pure and lovely, dwell on the fine, good things in others. Think about all you can praise God for and be glad about.

9) Keep putting into practice all you learned from me and saw me doing, and the God of peace will be with you.

12) I now know how to live on almost nothing or with everything. I have learned the secret of contentment in every situation, whether it be a full stomach or hunger, plenty or want;

13) for I can do everything God asks me to with the help of Christ who gives me the strength and power."

The great apostle wrote this passage while he was imprisoned in Rome... and as we've detailed before, if you were in prison in Rome, nothing was provided for you. Everything you needed (whether clothing, food, even writing materials) had to be brought in to you from someone on the outside.

After an unexplained dry spell where the church had been providing him with very little, they had stepped up the pace of helping meet his daily needs. This letter is Paul's thank you letter to them for their help and provisions.

But even in these dismal conditions and surroundings, Paul is writing. He is teaching, he is leading, and he is encouraging.

Through his words he is explaining to the church at Philippi, and down through the generations to us today, that living a non-anxious life, to be "anxious about nothing" as he states it, is a daily determination more than a destination. It is an exercise to be continued rather than a "one and done".

Step one in this path is learning to be grateful and giving God the thanksgiving he deserves for all that He has blessed us with.

It is important to note that Paul does not say, just stay the course, hang around the body of Christ, and you will wake up one day and be a more thankful person.

He says you must learn to be a person filled with grace...and many of us,...this preacher included...cannot begin to learn how strong grace is until we are faced with, and learn to grow through, a season of weakness brought about by trials.

It is hard to be thankful when you are living in fear and anxious about your future. The trick is to come to the understanding that we can silence fear by being and speaking out loud our gratefulness for our blessings. It is important to grasp the concept that anxiety goes down when thanksgiving goes up.

In this message Paul specifically tells us the value of being calm… and he speaks to us concerning every letter of that word…in order.

C….He tells us to first **celebrate** who God is and be thankful for all He has done for us.

A…Then he tells us through prayer and petition make our requests know to Him…to **ask**.

L…Then he invites us to **learn** to do as he has done and be able to find contentment in whatever situation we find ourselves…whether needy or plentiful.

M…Finally he recommends we keep our mind under control by **meditating** on all the things that are pure, lovely, honest and good that surround us every day.

There are many things in our socially connected world that foster anxiety like never before. Some surveys say that 70% of men and as much as 50% of the women in the world today suffer from anxiety.

Even with all of this connectedness, we feel more alone than ever. Thanks to sites like Facebook, Snapchat, and Tic Tok we are more aware of what others have (that maybe we don't) than ever before.

Thanks to global media, we are more aware of worldwide tragedies than ever before and are bombarded daily with bad, mostly useless, information.

Without some built-in buffer (think our relationship with the one who is on the throne and controls it all) we are at the mercy of anxiety and the constant state of "what if's". Therefore, anxiety increases as perceived control decreases.

Paul says come back to the gospel message and celebrate what we know to be true about God. To acknowledge that He is the same yesterday, today, and tomorrow and that He (not the circumstances) is still in control.

Paul tells us that peace, God's peace which passes all understanding, is found on a pathway paved with prayer.

Therefore, the more you pray specifically the more God can ease your anxiety personally. Know this…God is more eager to respond to prayer than we are to make these requests known to Him.

Paul breaks it down in order. Prayer. Petition. Request.
Approach Him through prayer standing in the full knowledge that He hears you and is able to help.
Petition His attention. Request His help.
And then finally, make you request known, ask for something specific, definite and definable.

When we pray in this manner, if helps us get to the root of the problem. Generalized prayer accomplishes nothing. "God bless my family"…he answer? Ok, exactly how?

1 Peter 5:6-7 states:
6) If you will humble yourselves under the mighty hand of God, in His good time He will lift you up.
7) Let Him have all your worries and cares, for He is always thinking about you and watching everything that concerns you.

This we know. We have a great big God. One who heals. One who restores. One who is able to use us in any given situation where we stand and say, "Here I am". As Hagar said, "He is the God who sees me!"…and He sees us beginning to end…warts and all. He knows our strengths and is quick to forgive our weaknesses.

There is nothing you can do that God can't fix if you let Him. His glory will shine in our inadequacies.

He even told the great apostle Paul, author of half the New Testament, "My grace is sufficient for you, for my power is made perfect in weakness."

He will never call anyone to accomplish a mission that he won't also equip to complete that mission.

Let us give Him praise and thanksgiving as we move forward into this next week, making our petitions known through prayer and requesting His attention and action.

Duty, Honor, and Courage

Occasionally, as your pastor, I am called to preach a message, as the Old Testament prophets were, that calls all of us to a higher sense of duty, honor, and courage.

Today is such a message.

In 2022, Eric Matazxas, whom you've heard me speak of many times, penned a book entitled "Letter to the American Church".

The purpose and subject matter of this book is to compare the current "Church" in America to the "Church" that existed in Germany during the early 1930's…and what it did….or more specifically did not do… as the Nazi Party rose to power and subsequently spread it's decidedly evil agenda across the country and into the world.

To bring the conversation quickly to a point, is to say the "Church", "Christ's church", mind you, was silent in the face of this evil in the 1930's of Germany and did absolutely nothing in the way of taking a stand against it.

Metaxas reasons in the writing of this slim volume, that the "Church", again, "Christ's Church" in America today is doing exactly the same thing…standing silent in the face of what by any means of the imagination should be labeled as "evil".

And I quote, "Though it may be a gruesome thing to consider, the monstrous evil that befell the civilized world precisely because of the German Church's failure is likely a mere foretaste of what will befall the world if the American Church fails in a similar way at this hour."

There is no question that for now, over 247 years, the entire world watches everything that concerns the Unites States of America. For most of the world we are "That shining city on a hill".

There is also no question that God, in His sovereignty, chose us to represent truth, justice, and liberty to the world. And if that same God has chosen the American Church to stand against the evils and deceptions of our present day, we had better be about the business of doing everything possible to fulfill our obligations.

Within the last 30 years or more, right here in America, we have seen the emergence and rapid growth of ideas and forces that are diametrically opposed to and are at war with God Himself.

This is all founded in Marxist "divide and conquer" ideology though to truly announce itself as such would wake up many people who are asleep.

We have all stood quietly by while acceptance of the LBGTQ+ agenda and its demand for equal rights under the law swept to the forefront of the American conversation. Today we see that "Critical Race Theory", "radical transgender", and "pro-abortion on demand" have quickly settled into their positions in our American culture without much, if any, challenge.

To speak out against any of these topics will welcome the speaker to a host of attacks…so many prominent pastors and clergy dodge the topics all together.

Many have done so because they have been persuaded by their church elders or even the congregation as a whole that to speak out is to somehow abandon the "Gospel message".

Yet these topics and positions all remain inescapably anti-God and anti-human.

In the Old testament, God called His hand-selected prophets to call His people to actually be the people of God…and not in name only. He called them to remember the Covenant He established with them and not wander off to worship the idols of the world. His part as the provider was to provide their needs, many times before they even asked, and their part was to remain resolutely attached to Jehovah God and His revealed presence.

Today, God is still calling His people…now known as the "Church" to do the same thing…to actually be the Church. To actually live out their faith so that all of society is blessed.

There are those that say to speak out on these subjects makes us "political" and involves us in topics where we should not be involved. I would ask where did these ideas come from that we should not tell the world what God says…in His word…about such topics.

Did Jesus not command His disciples to go and spread the word to the uttermost corners of the earth? I think He did. And I don't remember Him saying to water it down first…make it palatable…and politically correct.

I have said all of this so far this morning to say this:

God expects us to stand for what we know is right, truthful, and justified. He also expects us to stand (and not waiver) against what is not right, truthful, and justified.

We have that opportunity right now before us today.

In September 2022, a grass roots movement was begun in Newberry, Florida. A group came together to gather enough signed petitions to get a proposed amendment on the voting ballot next year.

This proposed amendment is called the "Human Life Protection" Amendment and reads:

"An amendment recognizing the God-given right to life of the preborn individual. Defines "preborn individual" as a preborn human person at any stage of development. Affirms that life-saving procedures to save the life of the mother shall not be construed as a violation when accompanied by reasonable steps to save the life of the preborn individual. To be added to the Declaration of Rights under Article 1 of the Florida Constitution."

I don't know how any of you feel about this topic. We have never discussed it in private…much less from the pulpit.
I can only tell you this, and to me the facts are staggering.

In 2022, there were 82,581 abortions performed in Florida.

With 33,010 abortions being reported in the first four months of 2023, Florida is on a pace to surpass 99,000 preborn lives terminated this year.

These numbers add to the nearly 4 million lives taken since 1973 in the state of Florida alone.

What do I think? I think we should join this fight and step up for those who cannot speak for themselves…those that are "fearfully and wonderfully made" **Psalm 139: 13-14**

I'm sure you've heard this before but it is worth repeating…. **Edmund Burke** was a statesman and political thinker in the British Parliament in the 1700's. He was also a follower of Martin Luther and supported the Reformation.

He was called the Father of Conservatism and is known for the following quote: **"The only thing necessary for evil to triumph in the world is for good men to do nothing"**.

It takes 891,000 plus signed petitions to get an amendment on the ballot.

Currently we are somewhere around 2% of goal.

So what am I asking?
If you agree that the right-to-life is God-given and should be protected:

1) I am asking you to personally sign a petition.
2) I am asking you to take some with you and ask your friends, neighbors, co-workers….any registered voter you can get in front of, to sign one as well.
3) If you run out of copies, make more and keep going.

The deadline to have these turned in and counted is six months away, February 1st.

This is not only our calling…it is our privilege to stand against those who place so little value on the life of an unborn child.

And we don't have a moment to spare.

The Transforming Effect of Loving Christ

John Chapter 20-21

John Chapter 20
30) "And truly Jesus did many other signs in the presence of His disciples, which are not written in this book;
31) but these are written that you may believe that Jesus is the Christ, the son of God, and that believing, you may have life in His name."

These verses constitute the goal and purpose for which John wrote his gospel...which is: to provide evidence for the deity and Messiahship of Jesus Christ, and that this evidence would lead one to believe, and by believing in Him, have eternal life through Him.

Now, from the spiritual high, that this chapter, ending in these verses produces, one would think this would end the gospel according to John.

I mean, where better to end this wonderful work?

Read the accounts. Come to a place of believing them...which is to say believing on Christ...and done! Eternal life awaits!

But like the television commercial beckons you... "Wait there's more!"

And in Chapter 21, John brings us all back to reality.

And he does it with none other than that "man about Christ", Peter. And this is not the Peter we will read about in the books of Acts. Nor is this the Peter we will study in I and II Peter later in the New Testament.

This is Peter with all his warts. This is hard-headed, self involved, most always on the wrong side of the law, making a mess of things Peter.

Chapter 21

1) After these things Jesus showed Himself to the disciples at the Sea of Tiberias, and in this way He showed Himself:
2) Simon Peter, Thomas called the Twin, Nathanael of Cana of Galilee, my brother James and I, (John) and two others of His disciples were together.
3) Simon Peter said to them, "I am going fishing."

Now it is important to note this is happening after the death, burial, resurrection, and revealing of Jesus Christ. And this is not Peter saying "I need a day off,...let's get a pole and go lay by the sea shore." This is Peter saying, "This is all a little hard for me to get my mind around, so I'm going back to what I know."

3 and 4) We'll come too, we all said. We did, but we caught nothing all night. At dawn we saw a man standing on the beach but couldn't see who it was. (paraphrased)

Commercial fishermen fish at night because the water is cooler after the sun goes down and many species approach the surface because of the temperature change.

5) Then Jesus called to them, "Children, did you catch any fish?"
"No" we replied.

6) Then He said, "Throw out your nets on the right-hand side and you'll get plenty of them!" and we did and couldn't draw in the net because of the weight of the fish there were so many.

Lesson Number One:

Here is the Lord making a statement to his beloved Peter and all of the other disciples. He is telling them that He controls the fish (and everything else).

You are no longer fishers of fish, but fishers of men. I alone have raised you up for this calling and hand selected you all.

7 and 8) Then I said to Peter, "It is the Lord" and immediately Peter was out of the boat swimming to shore while the rest of us pulled the loaded net back to shore.

9, 10, and 11) When we got there, we saw that a fire was kindled and fish were frying over it and there was bread. "Bring some of the fish you just caught," Jesus said, so Peter came out and dragged the net ashore. By his count there were 153 large fish and yet the net wasn't torn.

Lesson Number Two

When the Lord tells you to do something, he will always equip you for that task and see you through to completion.

12, 13 and 14) "Now come and have some breakfast," Jesus said, and none of us dared to ask Him if He was the Lord for we were quite sure of it. Then Jesus went around serving us the bread and fish. This was the third time Jesus had appeared to us after His resurrection.

Lesson Number Three

See Romans 8:28 "Nothing can separate us from the love of God." Here Jesus catches the disciples in a willful act of disobedience.

They had returned to their own understanding rather than following his instructions.

Can you imagine the conversation around that fire? The apologies? The embarrassment?

So how does Jesus disciple His disciples? How does He put them back on track? In what manner does He challenge them?

15 and following) "After breakfast, Jesus said to Simon Peter, 'Simon, son of Jonah, do you love Me more than these?'

"Yes," replied Peter, "You know that I do."

"Then feed my lambs," Jesus told him.

The Jesus repeated the question, "Simon, son of Jonah, do you love Me?"

"Yes, Lord, You know that I love You."

"Then tend My sheep."

And then He said a third time, "Simon, son of Jonah, do you love Me? This grieved Peter to be asked a third time and he answered, "Lord, you know all things; You know that I love you."

Jesus said again, "Then feed my sheep."

Lesson Number Four

Know this: If you are off course, headed in the wrong direction, doing the wrong things for the wrong reasons, Jesus will show up in your life when you least expect it.

These men were making their way back to shore after fishing all night and catching nothing. They were not rookies. They were master fishermen in their former lives and possibly had never encountered an entire night where they caught absolutely nothing. Little did they know, the heart ache would not end there, when they were surprised by their Rabbi, their Messiah, standing on the shore.

I'm sure we've all had that moment. That moment when the Lord catches us out of bounds. That moment when He asks the piercing question… "Ummmm…..just what are you doing?"

That one simple question we don't want Him to ask and the one we have no answer for.

Our hope is in these words: "And this is the will of God, that I should not lose even one of all those He has given me."

John 6:39

When the King of Kings and Lord of Lords should give us a dump truck of accusations and recriminations…he simply asks "Do you love Me more than these?"

What are "these" he speaks of? "These" are the things of your old life, your old way, led by the whims of the flesh. To Peter, He asks, "Peter, do you love me more than boats? Than anchors? Than nets? Than fishing?"

IMPLIED: "Haven't you seen enough?" "Haven't you heard enough?" "Are you really mine?" "Do you really love Me?"

ALSO IMPLIED: If so…then serve!

Put away your boat, Lay down your nets, give away your anchors,

and feed my sheep.

In short do what you have been called to do!

How much do you love the Lord?

When you've wasted your time and achieved nothing on your own, will you be ready to face Him once you've made it back to shore?

Sanctification is not going about your business as usual and waiting for the Holy spirit to fill you up in your spare time.

Sanctification is the relentless, on-going pursuit of the knowledge of the glory of Christ and all He has done…and is currently doing for us.

"Trust in the Lord with all your heart and lean not on your own understanding, in all your ways acknowledge Him and He will make your paths straight." **Proverbs 3:5,6**

John ends his gospel message with this story he received that day (along with the other disciples) from his Risen Lord.

He is in everything and everything is in Him. He has made everything and there is nothing that was made that is not of Him.

And all He asks is this.

Do you believe and do you love Me?

If so, be humble, be kind, and tend my sheep.

The Eyes of the LORD... Stop, Look, and Listen

Various passages

Proverbs 15:3
"The eyes of the Lord are everywhere, keeping watch on the wicked and the good."

In the second chapter of Exodus we read the story of an Israeli child, who was found (by Pharaoh's daughter) floating in the river in an ark made of bulrushes.

Pharaoh's daughter had compassion for him, took him into Pharaoh's house to raise, and gave him the name of Moses.

For those of you that are keeping score, she named him Moses because "I drew him out of the water."

When he was grown, as the story goes, he went out unto his brethren and saw an Egyptian taskmaster beating a Hebrew.

Verse 12) "And he looked this way and that way, and when he saw that there was no man looking, he slew the Egyptian, and hid him in the sand."

The passage tells us that this outburst of wrath (which would cost Moses forty years of his life as he fled to the wilderness to escape Pharaoh's punishment) came about because he looked "this way"…to the left, and "that way"…to the right, and seeing no one he believed the coast was clear.

What he failed to do is what you and I can easily forget to do: he never looked up.

Giving no thought to what his LORD would think about his actions, Moses took matters into his own hands.

He did a courageously right thing (helping a fellow Hebrew) in a devastatingly wrong way (killing an Egyptian taskmaster) and in the process, made a mess of things.

As we look at this simple story a little closer, we can see that living life by only looking left and right can keep us in a self-centered loop.

Also we only see a very narrow slice of life, much like the cart horses in St. Augustine.

Here, we are only seeing life with blinders on. We can only see, and therefore only react to, things from our own perspective and not the perspective we're meant to keep asking for…which is God's.

The bible is full of illustrations of tremendous mistakes (many made by God's chosen men) when they took their eyes away from God's chosen path and…after looking left and right, followed their own understanding straight into peril.

The key to living on earth is living in the light of our Father in heaven.

He sent His son to be the walking talking example of this when He said, "I am the light of the world, whoever follows me will not walk in darkness, but will have the light of life." **John 8:12**

In the Old Testament, we are told that in the coming age, the Messiah would be a light for all of Israel, as well as for the people of the whole earth.

Just as a pillar of fire and a pillar of smoke led the nation of Israel through the wilderness by day and night, Jesus is to be the light of life for those that follow Him.

In the early 1990's, at Calvary Reformed Church, in Holland, Michigan, a youth group leader named Janie Tinklenberg, began a grassroots movement to help the teenagers in her group remember a phrase she wanted at the forefront of everything they did. The phrase...What Would Jesus Do?...shortened to WWJD spread worldwide among the Christian youth who wore bracelets bearing these initials.

There is incredible power that comes from looking up and acknowledging the presence of God first---before (key word) we decide on any course of action in our daily lives.

How we treat our co-workers, how we treat our friends, how we treat our loved ones, in short, everything we do should first be brought under the lamp of God.

Our goal in life should be ending the separation between God and our daily lives by not only acknowledging, but embracing the fact that God in heaven is watching everything we do.

And this is not acknowledging God as the ultimate "Big Brother" that we see in most Communist regimes...this is the "Loving Father" who delights in making our paths straight when we submit to Him and not to our own understanding.

This is the act of sanctification. This is bending our will to the will of the Father. And for this action, He promises to pour out bountiful blessings on us from His infinite riches through His Son, Christ Jesus.

Our lives and relationships will take on and tap into rich new meanings, significance, and strength, directly proportional to our ability to look up at God and acknowledge His presence.

Yesterday's Sara Young's devotional, Jesus Calling, read: "Hold My hand and trust. So long as you are conscious of My presence with you, all is well. It is virtually impossible to stumble while walking in the Light with Me. I designed you to enjoy Me above all else. You will find the deepest fulfillment of your heart in Me alone."

So many people think of the God of heaven as a cranky old man sitting on His throne with a fly swapper in one hand and lightning bolts in another. A patriarchal "Santa Claus" just looking for a reason to take you off His list. This is not the God we serve.

Jeremiah 29:11 states, "For I know the plans I have for you," declares the Lord, "plans to prosper you and not to harm you, plans to give you hope and a future."

He does not set his mind to catch you in the act of sin and messing up. His heart toward you is steeped in love and grace. His desire for you is to look toward Him **before** your actions could hurt you and those you love the most.

Romans 2:4 tells us that it is through His very goodness, by the power of the Holy Spirit, that we are brought to repentance and redeemed.

How great a God we serve!

As we bask in His Presence, we grow in our desire not to do anything that could come between Him and us. It is in this place, with eyes on Him, that strength and confidence builds.

Psalm 34:17 "When the righteous cry for help, the Lord hears and delivers them out of their troubles. The Lord is near to the broken-hearted and saves the crushed in spirit."

If you have ever felt far from God, or have wanted to stay hidden from Him, He continues to stand beside you waiting for the day, the hour, the minute, of your return. He is the God of second, third, and thirty-fifth chances.

He is waiting for you to look up, to call upon His name, and find safety and refuge in Him…for right now, and for the future.

"The name of the Lord is a strong tower. The righteous run to it and are safe." **Proverbs 18:10**

You will find comfort in God's constant nearness and observation of your life, and that can't help but spill over into the way you graciously interact with others.

But even when you mess up as Moses did so long ago. Get up, dust yourself off and continue on keeping a closer eye on the things of God.

And remember, though Moses' decision cost him forty years in the wilderness, God still used him later in life in a mighty way.

Our God is the same today, tomorrow, and for the ages to come. He changes not and will use you, no matter your past, to bring glory to His name.

The decision, as always, is yours to make. Amen.

Distraction: Satan's Favorite Weapon

Last week we discussed the importance of "looking up" and keeping your eyes on God, rather than looking to the left and right, and then following your own understanding.

Today, we are going to look at one of Satan's favorite weapons: **Distraction**, and how you can know it for the problem that it is.

For our purposes, we will define **distraction** as: that which pulls you away from what is most important.

In the modern world today, we find a media-saturated society that is custom-fitted with daily distractions. We are bombarded every single minute of every single day with information from one source or another…and seldom is **any** of it as Paul says: "things that are true, honest, just, pure, of good report, full of virtue and praise".

When was the last time you turned on Fox News, CNN, or any other broadcast news station and found any of these things?
Next question: Do you not know this is intentional and by design?

The old newspaper slogan is still alive and well in media today.
"If it bleeds, it leads!" There is gold in them there hills and revenue in the advertising stream…and ratings drive the advertising revenue. More eyeballs…more money. It's just that simple.

Now enter the master of this world who is a schemer, liar, and a master at deception. He knows us better than we know ourselves. He is keenly aware of our weaknesses and the exact areas of our lives to attack and bring us to spiritual defeat.

For over four thousand years he has been in the business of **standing against** the children of God and attempting to do great harm to their witnesses and testimonies for the Lord Jesus Christ.

To do this he doesn't need to lead Christians astray from their core beliefs. All he needs to do is **distract** us from **seeking and maintaining** our daily personal relationship with Christ.

If he can fill our lives with world events, activities, pursuits, and pleasure, he knows we will have little time to spend with Christ and His written words.

With the burgeoning growth of social media, surveys have found that we spend upwards of **forty-seven percent** of our time thinking about something else rather than the moment we are in.

As we said, this is the definition of **distraction**, and as the apostle Paul said of sin, I have personally come to realize that I am the king of distraction.

I have realized just this week how much time I spend thinking and planning about what I am going to do next rather than whole-heartedly enjoying the moment I am in.

The devil can't make you sin…but what he can do is neutralize your witness when he is keeping you focused and busy on worldly things.

At some point we must unplug, take a deep breath, and realize our **attention** is our most important **commodity** and **must be protected.**

I ask you…what are you missing? What are you **distracted from** that you should be **devoted to**?

Step one is to **audit** the things in your life that is getting your **attention**. One of the things I have noticed this week is (with me personally) I simply need to **slow down**!

Captain Kirk was constantly asking Scotty for **more power**! As one who knows…you cannot "stop and smell the roses" as they say, at warp speed!

Studies show that the average person touches their cell phone screen 2,600 times a day…with heavy users clocking in at 5,400!

That adds up to 4.5 to 7 hours a day we spend on our phones.

Setting **priorities** for our daily lives has more to do with choosing what is **better or best** for us than what is specifically **right or wrong.**

What can **you do** to improve your daily walk with Christ? Where can you **choose better**? What **distraction** are you moving **from**? What **devotion** are you moving **to**?

Focusing your **attention on Him** is the beginning of your **devotion to Him**.

We have all seen the hashtags. "Follow me on Facebook", "Follow me on Instagram", "Follow me on Twitter".

Jesus simply says, "Here I am! I stand at the door and knock. If anyone hears my voice and opens the door, I will come in and eat with him and he with Me."

We can all learn a lesson from Nehemiah who the Lord tasked with leading Israel to rebuild the wall around the city after the nation returned from the Babylonian exile.

Although he faced opposition from without and abuse from within, Nehemiah steadfastly resolved to complete his "great work" and not be **tricked or distracted** from doing so.

Four times his enemies sought to pull him off the job and four times he said the same thing...**no**.

We should all learn this valuable single word sentence (**No!**) when the temptation of distraction is attempting to pull us off course.

The Lord is coming and many think "right soon."

This world is about the business of setting the stage for the coming Antichrist with its increasingly one world thought patterns. One world religion. One world Government. One world currency. One world environmentalism. This is the prop building, the arranging of the deck chairs, for what Jesus called "the beginning of the end".

Yet, one day, with no warning whatsoever the Lord will appear in the air and take his church with Him back to heaven in a nano-second. That will be the opening salvo for what will open the world to seven years of judgment and chaos. As it is written, we know it will be.

Until then, let us keep our eyes on Him, our attention where it needs to be, that He may find us doing His work when He returns.

In Matthew 24 and 25 Jesus teaches His disciples about the signs that will occur just prior to his return.

One of these signs to look for will be God's chosen people, the Jews, returning to the land God gave them, and the rebirth of Israel as a nation. This has already happened in May of 1948 when the world, led by the US, acknowledged Israel as a nation.

Jesus then told them that when you see these things know that I am near...even at the door!.

The clock is ticking. He is coming soon! Do not let the world as it is set and designed, **distract** you from **your** "great work". Be about His Father's business when Jesus returns!

Have your lamp trimmed and be at the edge of the clearing awaiting that wonderful day!

Amen

Sermon, July 16, 2023

July 4th and the Resurrection

On July 4th, we celebrated our country's 247th birthday when the Declaration of Independence was signed by 56 men of the Continental Congress. They pledged their lives, their fortunes, and their sacred honor.

We have all heard this story down through the years, in history classes across the nation. What I don't remember hearing is how the story ended for these 56 men. Did any of them face hardship? Was there sacrifice involved?

When you look further, you find that five signers were captured by the British forces, tried as traitors to England, tortured and killed.

Twelve of the signers had their homes ransacked and burned to the ground. The British couldn't find one of the signers, so they arrested his wife. She died in prison two months later. Two others lost their sons while they were serving in the Revolutionary Army. Nine more died from wounds or hardships of the war. Some, who enjoyed great wealth at the beginning of the war, died penniless.

These men put their lives on the line hoping for a better way of life for themselves and their families and friends.

They knew full well that by signing this document, the penalty would be death if they were captured. They were looking for independence and freedom and were willing to sacrifice all to obtain it.

Today, we will also celebrate Communion as we remember and worship our Risen Lord for his singular sacrifice and declaring our independence from the slavery to sin.

All during his three and a half years of ministry, Jesus continually told those around Him that, "My time has not yet come." But during the week of His crucifixion, He knew His time had come.

That week He entered the Temple and ran off those who had turned His Father's house of worship into a cheapened marketplace. He called out the religious leaders of the day for their lack of belief and hardened hearts. He called them vipers and white washed tombs. He made radical statements like "I am the true vine", "I am the light of the world", "I and the Father are one", and "I am the way, the truth and the light."

He came not to condemn the world but to save it. But make no mistake about it, He knew his statements and actions would be akin to voluntarily signing His own death warrant. Yes, Jesus knew all along, He would suffer and die.

But unlike the signers of the Declaration of Independence, there was nothing in it for Jesus. He was already God's Son. He was already there from the beginning. He already had a heavenly seat at the right hand of the Father. He already knew the glory and treasures of heaven.

Yet he came to earth, became flesh, and freely gave His life for us. He died for us for **our** sins, not His, to secure **our** freedom, not His.

This year as we celebrate the 4th of July, let us never forget the sacrifice our Jesus made for us.

As we enjoy communion with Him this morning as He instructed the apostles to do in remembrance of Him, let us as one, partake of the bread that represents His body given for us, and drink the wine that represents His blood that was shed for us.

And we do all this in thankfulness and worship of the one who said, "Whoever drinks of the water that I give him will never thirst again; as the water that I give him will become a well of water springing up to eternal life."

Please join me now as we remember:

"And as they were eating, Jesus took the bread and blessed it, telling them, 'Take, eat, this is my body that is given for you.'

And he took the cup and gave thanks, and gave it to them, saying, 'Drink all of it: for this is my blood of the new testament, which is shed for many for the remission of sin.'"

Father we thank you today for your plan to redeem man. We thank you for the courage, honor and obedience of your son Jesus who laid down His life so many years ago that we may know salvation. As one, we give blessings and honor and glory to your name.

Amen

Hope. . .The Real Thing

This past weekend, Cathy Karen and I had the fun adventure of a short ocean cruise aboard the MSC Seaside.

It was a three-night, four-day turnaround to their private island and we both had a wonderful time.

The private island is called **Ocean Cay** and is 20 miles south of Bimini. It is an artificial island built by a construction company in the 1960's where they mined for Aragonite sand for diverse industrial purposes.

The interesting part of this story is that environmental issues in the 1960's were practically unheard of, and once the company received their fill of the sand they needed, they packed up and left for home, leaving a wasteland behind.

Today, thanks to the efforts of MSC Cruise Line, it is a thriving, tropical paradise and **reestablished Marine Reserve**. During the process, MSC removed **seventy-five tons of refuge** from the small island, then brought in and planted **seventy five hundred shrubs, small trees, and palm trees.** Additionally, they relocated and nurtured back-to-life, **four hundred coral reefs around the island.**

There is much more to the MSC story, but we are not here today to lift up a cruise line.

I must tell you, however, that while spending some time in reading and quiet reflection aboard, the Lord **placed this on my heart and mind to share with you today.**

In my spirit, I heard Him say, "David, as you look out from this balcony and take in the beauty of this restored and refurbished island, I want you to understand that **this is the restoration I do whenever anyone comes to me in repentance by faith.**

I am not in the **white-washing business**. I am not interested in just making things, as they are, a little better. I gave my life on a cross and was then resurrected and restored by the word of My Father. I have been reborn to become **the first fruit of all who will follow me**. My program is not a make over. **My program is the resurrection of the dead.**

If Scripture teaches us anything, It's that in God's hands, **dead things come back to life.** You can't undo your past, but there's always **hope for a new life and a new beginning**. The word **hopelessness** can't be found in God's dictionary.

"For I have plans for you", declares the Lord, "Plans to prosper you and not to harm you, plans to give you hope and a future."

Jeremiah 29:11

This wasn't the prophet Jeremiah delivering a message of **shame and abandonment, but rather hope,** to the wayward nation of Israel. **"This is our God. This is what He does. He loves us",** to quote a current gospel radio hit.

"Now **faith** is the assurance of things hoped for, the conviction of things not seen." **Hebrews 11:1**

By faith, we have all been reborn to a living, thriving hope for the future through the resurrection of Christ our Lord. His work within us is not simply **rearranging the deck chairs on our cruise ship** and calling it a day.

Through Christ, we are a new creation, set apart. A refurbished, **remade, diamond that shines within the ocean of waste we call the world.**

As our ship approached this tiny spit of land, I was amazed how it dazzled in the distance. I felt the Lord telling me, "**This is how I see you, and all those the Father has given me,** whenever I look your way. **Gone is the unwanted debris, clear of leftover trash, and I rejoice in the new and shining creation standing before me.**"

Life for the first century believer was anything but easy. They were hunted and persecuted everywhere they went.

They were hassled by the **non-believing scoffers**, by the **pagan Roman Empire**, and even by their own **religious leaders** who refused to believe that Christ was indeed, the Messiah.

Without their **hope** in the promise of the future eternal life with Christ, they had little support and empathy to draw from. Then, and now two-thousand years later, **where there is no faith in the future, there is no hope.**

Hope then becomes the future tense of faith.

In I and II Peter we hear from a far different Peter than the one we came to know in the gospels. **It is thirty-two years later. This Peter** is older and wiser than the impetuous, hot-headed, Peter of before. **Seasoned,** would be a good word to apply to this elder Peter…

and as he wrote, he knew his death through martyrdom was just ahead.

So what were his closing thoughts as his ministry was coming to an end. What did he want his fellow believers to know?

In I Peter, Peter calls the church to be **known for doing good, for being helpful, and beneficial to the community.** He calls them, and through them down to us today, **to live God-honoring lives in a hostile environment. He challenges us** "to be holy as He is holy". **1 Peter 1:16**

Simply put, we have a Father who is holy, and as His children, we are to be like Him. Stripped down further, we find that to be **"holy"** is to live **"set apart"** in some exclusive and special way.

A good example of that is **"holy matrimony"** where a man and a woman are **"set apart"** leaving all others behind as they bond exclusively to each other.

As Christians, we too, have been **"set apart"** by confessing our belief in Christ as the living son of God, whose sacrifice washed our sins away. This established us as a **new creation** and allowed us to be called the **"sons of God"** and the **"bride" of Christ.**

In II Peter, he tells us that our gracious God **gives us everything** we need to grow in every part of our lives as we represent Him to a lost world.

Here, Peter finally **"gets it"** as one might say. No longer do we hear the old Peter saying, **"Step aside, Lord…I got this!".** This older, wiser, spirit-filled Peter knows there is nothing he can add **to what God has already done…what He has already provided.**

He encourages all of Jesus' followers to **continue in the faith** and **grow in the service to God** as we prepare for Christ's return. He calls us **to live out the purpose of our lives in Christ.**

In his book, **Hope Again**, Chuck Swindoll quotes the great Bible teacher James M Gray, who asks, **"Who can mind the journey when the road leads home?"**

And we know home is where the Lord is, for whoever believes.

Do you know how scarce hope is to those without Christ? They imagine a few given years of life and then into the utter darkness you go. **No** past. **No** present. **No** future.

Many of those same people define our insistence of a future eternal life as a pathological belief in the impossible. Much to their loss, they neither acknowledge nor believe in the eternal soul.

To them, death is simply the end of the line…everybody off the bus.

Be we have a **"living hope through the resurrection of Jesus Christ from the dead"** as Peter puts it. And with that comes a permanent inheritance **"imperishable and undefiled"**. Halleluiah!

Aren't you glad we're on this side of the fence versus those without knowledge or hope?

We have an unseen Savior who has gone before us to **"prepare a place for us so that where He is we may be also"**. **John 14:2**

Knowing this, we can be **content** in any situation that we find ourselves as we realize God has already provided everything we need for our present happiness and our future life to come.

Cathy Karen was amazed at the choices upon choices presented on the cruise ship's buffet. God would have you to know that the biggest buffet you an imagine here on earth, would pale to insignificance when compared to the coming **"Marriage Supper of the Lamb"** to which we all are invited.

Boiled down to it's smallest measure we say, "Our Lord lives!…and our **hope** is in Him! Hope for today, tomorrow, and all of eternity!"

With that I'd like to close in a prayer I've borrowed from Chuck's book:

"Father, words of **hope** and **encouragement** and **purpose** can really fall flat if things aren't right in our lives. If we aren't **right with you**, somehow these words seem meaningless. But when we **change our minds, when we turn around, when we truly and honestly repent,** we **hear with new ears**. Then, rather than resenting these words, we appreciate them more and **love you** and **worship you for them**.

Give us Your grace to match life's trials. Give us a sense of **hope, purpose**, and **encouragement** beyond our pain, in whatever form that comes. Give us **fresh assurance** that we are not alone, but rather the blessed children of a living God.

Let us never forget that **every jolt** in this rugged journey from earth to heaven is a reminder that we're on the right path.

Please show us how to **walk by faith** and embrace your beautiful plans for us. Plans to prosper us and not harm us."

Go with us now, Lord as we break bread together. Bless the hands that prepared it and this food we are about to receive to the nourishment of our bodies.

And I ask all of this in Jesus name. Amen.

Do You Know How Blessed We Are?

Joshua Chapters 3 and 4

My question for you today is: Do you know how blessed we are?

Many would answer that question by saying, "Absolutely!…we live in the United States of America and have been blessed by God with bountiful abundance and freedom that no other country in the world enjoys."

I would find it hard to argue with that answer…but it's not the one I'm looking for.

Maybe I should restate the question and add the word "spiritually": Do you know how spiritually blessed we are?

Certainly, there would be a multitude of correct answers to that question as well.

But at the bottom of it all, no matter your answer, part of it should include the following:

We are spiritually blessed beyond measure because we, this group, this time, in all the history of the world, have the totality of God's written word in our hands to lead and guide us as we live our daily lives.

Our Father in heaven used 40 different men over 1500 years to write 66 books of seamless history...and we have it all at our fingertips.

All relevant...not only to each other, but now, thousands of years later, this book is provided for us that we may live in the knowledge and will of God, and come to know His Son, Jesus the Christ as Messiah.

Today we are going old school in the Older Testament and we're going to look at the book and story of Joshua...and we are going to see how this section of the word of God speaks to us today as we, the Church, follow the risen Christ of the Newer Testament.

We're going to see how the God we serve stitched this book together... for as the apostle Paul said in his letter to Timothy, "to be profitable for instruction, for conviction of sin, for correction of error and restoration to obedience, and instruction in righteousness, which is, behaving honorably with personal integrity and moral courage, both in public and in private".

2 Timothy 3:16 The Amplified Study Bible

If you want to know why, read on.

All this, "so that the men of God may be complete and proficient, outfitted and thoroughly equipped for every good work".

2 Timothy 3:17 The Amplified Study Bible

This is the purpose and value of the book we call The Holy Bible.

In the Older Testament, at this time in the story of His chosen nation Israel, there were only three places to be.

You were either in **captivity** (Egypt), you were **wandering in the wilderness** (and hopefully becoming properly prepared), or you now ready and being blessed by entering the **"promised land"**.

Right away we see the comparison in our lives today.

Each and every one of us today, are either living in **captivity** (characterized by unrepentant sin), wandering in the **wilderness** (which is living a life outside of the will of God) or **on our way to the promised land** (living a life of obedience under the shed blood of Jesus Christ and the forgiveness of sin found only in Him).

You should know well the story of Joshua. He was 'the next man up" as they say in pro football. Moses, who was used by God to steal the nation from Pharaoh's hand, and lead them on their journey to freedom, had died.

The Lord God Jehovah then chose Joshua, as the time had now come, to lead them into the land God had promised to give them.

Their time in the wilderness had come to an end. God had washed the slavery and rebellion out of them and knew the time was right for them to experience the reward He had set aside just for them.

All nations great and small progress through the following sequence: They move from bondage to spiritual faith, from spiritual faith to a time of great courage, from great courage to liberty and from liberty to abundance.

We see this sequence played out again and again by the nation of Israel in the books of the Older Testament. We have also seen this sequence played out in our own country, The United States, a country that was founded in great courage by God-believing, God -honoring men.

Unfortunately, the sequence never seems to end in abundance, with everyone living happily ever after.
An excellent question would be, "Why not?"

As the sequence continues to evolve, the nation inevitably moves from abundance into complacency. Complacency then begins a death spiral as complacency leads way to apathy, apathy to dependence, and dependence returns the nation to bondage.

Gone is the faith, courage, liberty, and abundance that made the nation great. Gone are the times that the world saw them as a "city shining on a hill".

It is no stretch of the imagination that our great nation has become apathetic…toward God, His principles, and His instructions. With all the blessing God has bestowed on this nation, we now take it all for granted, and seldom take time to acknowledge Him at all. We have become believers in entitlement.

In America today **"normalcy bias"** rules…which is to say, "This is America! This is the way it was, this is the way it is, and this is the way it will continue to be!"…with the unspoken part of that being, no matter what we do or how we ignore the things of God.

The Lord had a word for a nation like that in His letter to the church in Laodicea, **Revelation, Chapter 3, verses 15 and following**: "I know you well, you are neither hot nor cold. I wish that you were one or the other! But since you are merely lukewarm, I will spit you out of my mouth!

You say, 'I am rich with everything I want; I don't need a thing!' and you don't realize that spiritually you are wretched and miserable and poor and blind and naked."

This is the word of the Lord to America today:

My advice to you is that you buy pure gold from me, gold purified by fire…only then will you be rich. And to purchase from me white garments, clean and pure, so you wont be naked and ashamed; and to get medicine from me to heal your eyes and give you back your sight."

And now for the good news! Instead of descending into bondage and completing the sequence, America can once again, turn her hearts and minds toward the Lord and be restored!

There has never been a greater need for revival in America than now! Revival in the people becomes revival in the churches which becomes revival in the communities. Revival in the communities becomes revival in the states which becomes revival in a nation.

And rest assured, true revival in America will become revival in Congress, revival in the House of Representatives, and revival in the Oval Office!

Restoration of America is possible and must be pursued to the glory of the Father who says, "Then, if my people who are called by my name will humble themselves and pray and seek my face and turn from their wicked ways, I will hear from heaven and will forgive their sins and restore their land." **2 Chronicles 7:14**

We as a nation must call each other to an on-going commitment of self-examination and repentance, turning from sinful behavior and re-aligning our lives with the will of God.

As we do this, we will stand on God's promise to bring healing and restoration to our nation. "And your ears shall hear a word behind you saying, 'This is the way, walk in it." **Isaiah 30:21**

I know you are thinking what can I do?...I am only one person.

You can begin today to pray for revival in our land. I know the Lord has laid this on my heart and I am praying for Him to make this a possibility right here in Green Cove Springs. We are part of a 27 church organization known as the Black Creek Baptist Association and I have brought it before them to come together and put together what could become the largest three day revival our county has ever seen...a three day event in the Cattlemen's Arena on the fair grounds.

It seats 3,000 and Cathy Karen and I are claiming that for God in prayer every night when we exercise by walking the parking lot of the fair grounds.

I am asking you to join us in this effort. There are many hurdles to jump to get this done, but I am more convinced than ever that it can and will be done.

Let's close in prayer.

Father God,

To your glory. To the glory of the Son. To the glory of the Holy Spirit. We pray today that Green Cove Springs and our 27 church organization will come alive in revival if we humble ourselves, if we pray, and if we seek your face.

Father, we ask You to bless this endeavor, remove all obstacles, provide the funding, and receive the glory and honor to Yourself, the One who is so worthy.

Father we ask that you work in the hearts and minds of the Black Creek leadership team as they pray over the decision to join together with us in this endeavor.

We thank you Lord for inclining you head and hearing our prayers today. We receive this from you by faith and we thank you for it.

In the precious name of Jesus, Amen.

Our God is Greater Than. . .

In The 1970's, Lee Strobel was a young, up-and-coming beat reporter for the Chicago Tribune. He was acknowledged for his investigative work and his articles were already winning awards.

I'm sure he envisioned one day seeing his name mentioned in the same circles as Bob Woodward who worked for the Washington Post and broke the Watergate story, which ended the presidency of Richard M. Nixon.

A devout atheist, life was moving along at a rewarding pace, and he lived this life unencumbered by the guilt-trip restraints he so sharply believed were presented by organized modern religion.

He found the entire narrative of Christianity to be nothing but campfire stories that had been shared down through the ages to control the uneducated. A side bar to this, he thought, was a carefully crafted and veiled plan to get into the financial pockets of these same misled and hood-winked people.

Life in the Strobel household was good. His wife had no religious connection, she was healthy and pregnant with their second child, and they were raising their first child to believe as they did.

Lee had it on auto pilot and it was working like clockwork, nothing to see here imaginary God, so move along, move along.

And then one fateful night, everything changed.

The Strobel's were dining out at their favorite restaurant and as was the practice, his young daughter was rewarded for finishing her meal with a nickel for the gum ball machine.

Very quickly, the evening changed for the worst as she swallowed the gum ball whole and it became lodged in her throat. Without the quick action of a registered nurse at the next table, the child would have been lost.

Lee and his wife were quick to acknowledge the nurse's actions with gratitude and were thankful for the wonderful coincidence of her being on-hand and close by.

"This wasn't a coincidence," she said, "My husband and I discussed many different restaurants tonight, but I felt a strong presence that God was leading us here."

"I didn't know why at the time, but I do now."

To fast forward the story, Lee's wife Leslie, embarked on a spiritual journey with this newly-acquainted devout Christian nurse, that led her to accept Jesus as Lord and Savior, invite Him into her life, and get baptized.

Lee was beside himself! In his mind, his wife had betrayed him and ruined their marriage. He had not signed on for this and told her straight up that he would not be around two years from then arguing with her about this new found "faith" that he abhorred.

"People created God and this narrative of a Savior because they are afraid of death", he shouted. "Either get your head straight, or we are done!"

Then out the door he went to spend time with a few former staff writers. Older men he considered mentors, and mentors who just happened to believe exactly as he did concerning Christianity.

He did not expect to hear what he was told. "You're an investigative reporter", said one, "Chase the leads, discover the facts, analyze the evidence, and write the story, win, lose, or draw!".

This was a watershed moment in the young life of Lee Strobel. He immediately set out to systematically prove, without a shadow of a doubt, that the entire story, soup to nuts, was a house of cards and a fabricated fairy tale. There was no way this "Jesus story" as presented in the bible would stand up to close scrutiny. He would discover the misrepresentations and impossibilities, catalog his findings, present her with these newly revealed facts, and get his wife back.

Fast forward again, two years later and Lee has chased every lead, conducted many personal interviews, examined the evidence and has ended up believing what millions have, since the coming and short life of the one they call Yeshua…Jesus.

This is where his investigation led him:

That Jesus is the Christ. The prophesized One, The Messiah.

That He gave His life for us on the cross that we may know salvation instead of the damnation that we deserve.

That He was dead and buried only to be resurrected from the dead three days later.

That in doing so He has conquered death and the fear of judgment to become the first fruit of many who will follow Him into eternity.

That this resurrection from the dead, as he bodily walked the earth again, was reported and recorded by more than five hundred witnesses in eight different appearances

And that his closest followers were eye-witnesses to His ascension into heaven forty days later.

Finally, he discovered that these same disciples, save one, followed Him in laying down their lives for the cause...certainly something no one would do when they secretly knew it to be an elaborate hoax.

All of these undeniable facts Lee discovered in his two year investigation which led him to the quiet announcement, "You win, God, you win."

It also cannot be overlooked or discounted in the telling of this story that all the while Lee was fighting the windmill and resisting the call God had placed on his family, that his wife, a newly-minted believer was praying for him every day, even though she seldom knew where he was or what he was doing.

Just beginning to fully understand the narrative and working her way through the bible for the first time, she prayed many passages over Lee as he continued to be frequently absent from the home.

One of her favorites was **Ezekiel 36:26-27,** "I will give you a new heart and put a new spirit in you; I will remove your heart of stone and give you a heart of flesh. I will put my spirit within you and cause you to walk in my statutes, and you will keep my ordinances and do them."

Today, Lee is seventy-one years old and has spent most of his adult life in the service of the Lord. He pastored the church where his wife came to know the Lord from 1987 to 2000.

His journey has taken him to ministry posts in California and now in Texas where he is a teaching pastor at Woodlands Church, in The Woodlands, Texas.

In 1998 he compiled his research done so many years before in a book entitled, "The Case for Christ: A Journalist's Personal Investigation of the Evidence for Jesus". To date it has sold multiple millions of copies worldwide.

I fully realize that I've spent more time this morning story telling than I have preaching.

The point of all of it is this. For those that are willing to open their eyes and hearts to hear it, the case for Christ is irrefutable.

Our bible is by far the greatest book ever written, the greatest story ever told, culminating in God loving us so much that he became one of us (in the form of Jesus).

He then laid down His life and shed His precious blood to create that narrow road whereby we may be saved from the consequences of our sins and become his redeemed children for all eternity.

There is a reason that to date **over five thousand** ancient **hand-written** manuscripts and fragments of manuscripts have been found of the Holy Bible. Second place numbers around nine hundred copies for Homer's epic poem The Iliad.

There is a reason that to date, the Holy Bible is the best selling book the world has ever known and has sold over **five billion** copies. This is **forty percent** more than the second place Quran.

And there is a reason why a beer-guzzling, take-no-prisoners, dedicated atheist journalist like Lee Stobel can have his entire life changed in an instant and become a follower and not a scoffer of the Word of God.

The reasoning behind all of this exists in two words and those words are **truth**.

God's word is **truth** and His love for us knows no bounds and endures forever.

I will close with the following:
Matthew 7: 7-8 (from the Amplified Bible)

"Ask and keep on asking and it will be given you; seek and keep on seeking and you will find; knock and keep on knocking and the door will be opened to you.

For everyone who keeps on asking receives, and he who keeps seeking finds, and to him who keeps on knocking, it will be opened."

No matter who you are, no matter where you are, no matter what you've done, God is greater than it all. He loves you and He has a plan for your life.

He stands "at the ready" to open up the treasure chests of heaven and pour out His blessings on those that will hear, believe, and follow.

He and he alone, is the one who can change your life forever through the completed work of Christ, and by the power of the Holy Spirit.

Only He can begin a new work in you and have you on the path of becoming a new creation in Christ Jesus.

A warrior for the faith, destined for the kingdom.

Amen.

Source: The Pure Flix Motion Picture, The Case for Christ

Will You Be Left Behind?

At 8:45 am, on a clear Tuesday morning, September 11, 2001, an American Airlines Boeing 767 loaded with passengers and 20,000 gallons of jet fuel, slammed into the north tower of the World Trade Center in New York City.

Television cameras were broadcasting what was initially thought to be a freak accident, when suddenly, 18 minutes later, a second Boeing 767, this time United Air Lines Flight number 175, turned sharply toward the World Trade center and sliced into the south tower near the 60th floor.

By now, it was immediately clear that America was under attack by unknown forces…forces that were incredibly using our own domestic airlines as weapons of mass destruction against us.

As millions watched the events unfolding in New York, another plane, American Airlines Flight 77 circled over Washington, DC, before crashing into the west side of the Pentagon military headquarters at 9:45 am.

15 minutes after this, we gasped as the television coverage from New York recorded the catastrophic collapse of the south tower in a massive cloud of smoke and dust.

30 minutes later, the north tower collapsed as well and thousands of lives were lost in an instant.

Finally, as the day's horror continued, we were advised of yet another high-jacked plane, United Airlines Flight 93, that was making a u-turn in it's light path, and headed back to the same area.

This plane, however never reached it's intended target, as a group of brave Americans overtook the terrorist flight crew and crashed the plane in rural Pennsylvania…surrendering their lives in the balance, but saving an untold multitude in the process.

Throughout the ensuing months, investigation after investigation emerged with the same findings…and those findings can be encompassed in one word…denial.

No one, absolutely no one, truly believed the following:

* ** That a group of nineteen known terrorists, many on world-wide watch lists, could enter the United States and move about without their every move and action being accounted for and analyzed.
* ** That some of this same group could enter FAA approved commercial aircraft flight training in Arizona.
* ** That these, involved in training, would discontinue the training course after they were professionally trained in takeoff operations…without also completing the sections on landing these commercial aircraft.
* ** That they would then all gather in Miami beach and vacation for three weeks, indulging themselves with every hedonistic activity they pleased, until the day before Sept 11.
* ** That they could smuggle small weapons past security into four separate airports, and successfully commandeer four commercial flights for their evil purposes.

No one believed at the time that any of this could happen…and not only happen but succeed. But as we all now know, it did.

And it all happened right under our noses, ignoring all the signs that something was coming that would forever change history as we know it in America.

With that in mind, this morning I want you to imagine a moment coming soon that will change everyone and everything, not only in the U.S., but all over our planet.

Imagine the same circumstances as on September 11th. Everyone going about business as usual, conducting their affairs, scurrying around, eating, drinking, marrying, and giving in marriage, celebrating birthdays, battling sickness, and involved in every other aspect of modern life.

People will be getting up, going to bed, working or playing, enjoying their pleasures or vices. No sweat… "just another day in paradise" as is often quoted.

I try to imagine these things happening all over the world. Will it be another bright and sunny day as it was in New York on September 11th?…or cloudy and overcast? Will the sun be rising or setting when the Moment comes that will change everything?

And I wonder what those of us who call themselves Christians will be doing on that day? Will they be as surprised as everyone else when the Rapture occurs? Or will they be eager, ready, and waiting?

Can you see the masses moving as usual? Millions walking about the streets of New York, Tokyo, New Delhi, Moscow, worried about their money, wondering about their relationships, anxious about their images on social media, following others on Twitter, Tik Tok, while checking the latest sports scores.

It will be just another day or night here on planet earth---until suddenly it isn't.

One day soon, the world will face the Great Disappearance where billions of people will be gone in a flash. This will be more powerful than a simultaneous world wide nuclear explosion, yet silent!...and invisible!

Every single follower of Jesus Christ gone! All of the children under the age of accountability gone! Along with all of the Christians who have preceded us in death!

Patients will disappear from their beds, babies from their cribs and children from their classrooms. Driverless vehicles will still be flying down the interstate, planes will suddenly be missing the flight crews, passenger trains at speed will have no engineers to be found.

The world will instantly be gripped by thousands of conspiracy theories in the aftermath of the Rapture. Global panic will pave the way for a one-world government which will ultimately lead to the emergence of an iron-fisted ruler and the onset of the seven year Tribulation.

It will be a day and time of utter chaos on an unimaginable scale for those that are "left behind".

This moment, this coming event, should be at the forefront of the mind of every Christian believer...especially as it pertains to the millions upon millions who will be "left behind".

If you have your bibles, turn to **Matthew 24:36-39**

"But of that day and hour no one knows, not even the angels of heaven, but My Father only. But as the days of Noah were, so also will the coming of the Son of Man be. For as in the days before the flood, they were eating and drinking, marrying and giving in marriage, until the day that Noah entered the ark, and did not know until the flood came and took them all away, so also will the coming of the Son of Man be."

Right now, the door to salvation is wide open, just like the door to the ark. The saving grace of Jesus Christ is still available to all…the free gift by the mercy of God the Father completed by His Son's sacrificial death at Calvary so long ago.

The question of today is…Have we, the collective body of Sharon Baptist Church done our level best to reach the world with the gospel before it's too late?

Until He leads me elsewhere, I am convinced that the Lord is impressing upon me…and through me to you…the need for spiritual revival in Sharon Baptist Church, the need for spiritual revival in the Black Creek Baptist Association and it's 27, soon to be 28 churches, the need for spiritual revival in Clay County, all over the State of Florida, the United States of America…and from there to the world.

There are many who believe that another Great Awakening is coming …the definition of that being: a time of great spiritual revival and an extra large and powerful out-pouring of our Father's Holy Spirit.

Many scholars agree that there have been four Great Awakenings in the Continental United States…the first one, dating back to the early 1700's, with the last one possibly beginning at the end of World War II and carrying over into the 60's and 70's. Each of these Great Awakenings was punctuated by earnest prayer, fasting, and self-evaluation by the saints of Christ. What followed were great revival movements calling down the Spirit of God and emphasizing the need for personal spiritual rebirth.

Millions came to know Jesus as Lord during these times of great revival and it can happen…all over again…today!

We should be on our knees "Praying it through" as the old timers believed.

There is little doubt that we are living in the age of scoffers. Instead of "Pride" their banners should read "Denial".

2 Peter 3:3 and following reads:
3) "Knowing this first, that there shall come in the last days scoffers walking after their own lusts.
4) And saying, 'Where is the promise of His coming? For since the fathers fell asleep, all things continue as they were from the beginning of creation."

And Jude 1:17 and following:
17) "Dear friends, remember what the apostles of our Lord Jesus Christ told you, that in the last times there would come these scoffers whose whole purpose in life is to enjoy themselves in every evil way imaginable.
18) They stir up arguments; they love the evil things of the world; they do not have the Holy Spirit living in them."

There is a laundry list of groups today that qualify for all of the above.

They deny God, Christ and the Holy Spirit. They consider the Holy Bible a books of fables and children's stories. They place themselves atop their man-made thrones.

We however are called to live our lives separate unto God, clinging to the word of God and Jesus our redeemer...as we venture out into the world, making disciples, and baptizing them in the name o the Father, the Son, and the Holy Spirit.

In closing I'd like to pray over us
Father God, we praise you, we honor you, we humble ourselves before you. Holy, Holy, Holy, are you Lord God and worthy to be praised are YOU.

Father, we acknowledge Christ as Savior and Redeemer. We call out to Him as Lord of all including our lives, for He and He alone is the King of all Kings, the Lord of all Lords.

In Jesus name, Father we ask that you bring a spirit of revival to the body of Sharon Baptist Church gathered here today.

Place in our hearts and minds, Lord, a burden for those that we know that will most likely be "left behind" on that great day of the coming of our Lord as He meets us in the sky and we are forever welcomed into the kingdom of God.

Help us not hold our tongues but guide them with love and compassion toward the truth that as your word says, "to come into the knowledge of the will of God" in their lives and families.

Help us be guided by the Holy Spirit to snatch them out of the hands of the enemy and bring them into the kingdom of God.

Go with us now as we leave this place and anoint us with your spirit to deliver the message…Jesus Christ is Lord of all…the truth, the way, and the life to come…for today and evermore…Amen.

Afterword

As always, it has been our distinct pleasure to host you on another guided tour through the land of Scattered Thoughts.

Were it up to us, you could all stay seated for a little while longer...we could refresh your drinks, and extend our time of fellowship.

But alas, the booking agent earns his keep and another group is patiently waiting at the dock to board.

On behalf of our crew and the entire publishing team, we'd like to wish you the best the rest of this year has to offer and a wonderful, fulfilling, blessed, and prosperous New Year.

Until next time.

DM

Special Thanks

To **Dale Tumelson**, my friend, my editor, who takes my Scattered Thoughts and molds them into something readable...no matter how many times I make the same grammatical errors.

To **Ralph Puckhaber** and **Jan Cammarata**, also my friends, who did the impossible and retrieved this entire book after it had been deleted during a storm.

They truly saved the day...and this book!

And to all the great pastors, teachers, and scholars that I listen to on the radio every day. Without their knowledge, direction, and inspiration, none of this would be possible.

John MacArthur   Chuck Swindoll   Alistair Begg
Jeff Shreve   Tony Evans   David Jeremiah
Greg Laurie   Richard Ellis

Lastly, to **Bill Swicegood,** who I'm fairly certain owes me money.

The Beatles were right about one thing...it all comes together "With a Little Help From My Friends".